What People Are Saying About
Harnessing Courage

Harnessing Courage is a touching story about the life of a remarkable young woman. In her middle school years, Laura Bratton became aware that she was going blind. She gives us a telling illustration not only of how she coped with her physical disability but also her growing awareness that, with courage and focus (grit) and thankfulness for love and support (gratitude), she could lead a wonderful, productive life. She shares these deep lessons with us so we all might grow mentally, physically, and spiritually.

Every school student who has to overcome large and small obstacles in life could benefit from reading Laura Bratton's courageous story.

RICHARD W. RILEY
Former U. S. Secretary of Education
Former Governor of South Carolina

Laura Bratton tells the inspiring story of how her perseverance, courage, and determination, and ultimately the love and support from family and friends, helped her overcome insurmountable obstacles at the onset of vision loss at an early age. Laura's unique life experiences, from being the first student with a visual impairment at Princeton Theological Seminary to being the first female pastor with a disability at her United Methodist Church, provide an insightful look into the important role that grit and gratitude play in leading an independent, meaningful, and fulfilling life. I had the opportunity to witness Laura's intelligence, motivation, and tenacity during her time as an undergraduate researcher in my lab at Arizona State University. Laura's story of overcoming massive obstacles is truly an inspiration for all of us as we attempt to handle adverse experiences in our lives. Laura describes her questions and conflicts over identity, spirituality, and empowerment, and provides her perspective and lessons learned in facing these issues. Readers will be moved by Laura's achievements, stirred by her wisdom, and prepared to harness courage during times that test our will.

SETHURAMAN 'PANCH' PANCHANATHAN
Executive Vice President, ASU Knowledge Enterprise; Chief Research and Innovation Officer, Arizona State University, Tempe

Laura Bratton has written a remarkable book that shows how she is so well qualified to help others overcome trauma and loss. Though the book is a story of loss, it is even more a story of courage and of how to accept the love of others, how to be sufficient and not dependent, and how not to complain. Laura did her graduate studies at Princeton Theological Seminary during my tenure there. She and her wonderful guide dog, Jira, enriched our lives in ways we will never forget, and she taught us far more than we ever gave her. Please read her story and give thanks to God.

IAIN R. TORRANCE
President Emeritus, Princeton Theological Seminary; Pro-Chancellor, University of Aberdeen, Scotland; Dean of the Chapel Royal in Scotland, Dean of the Order of the Thistle

Laura Bratton's powerful book equips each reader to overcome life's difficulties with grit and gratitude. She shows us how to live with meaning and purpose regardless of the challenges we face. I recommend this book to young and old alike.... It will touch your heart, mind, and soul.

PHILLIP FULMER

Hall of Fame Football Coach, University of Tennessee

Laura Bratton has written an inspiring story of true grit and steadfast faith, a moving testimonial that is sure to give encouragement to anyone facing obstacles in life. I'm grateful for this book.

WILL WILLIMON

Professor of Christian Ministry, Duke Divinity School; United Methodist bishop, retired

Harnessing Courage is a remarkable story of determination, perseverance, and strength. Laura Bratton's candid honesty will inspire readers to face adversity in their own lives with grit and gratitude. Whether it be a disability, tragedy, or affliction of any kind, the themes highlighted in this book are applicable to anyone needing encouragement. Laura is a guiding light to us all.

BILL HAAS

Professional golfer

There are no shortcuts to courage, it's true. But *Harnessing Courage* offers much hope and clarity.

PERRY TUTTLE

Clemson University Football Hall of Fame, First Round NFL Draft Pick; author; executive leadership coach

Harnessing Courage

Overcoming Adversity with Grit & Gratitude

Laura Bratton

Clovercroft Publishing

Harnessing Courage: Overcoming Adversity with Grit and Gratitude

Published by Clovercroft Publishing, Franklin, Tennessee

Published in association with Larry Carpenter
of Christian Book Services, LLC
www.christianbookservices.com

Edited by Robert Irvin

Cover and Interior Design by Suzanne Lawing

Printed in the United States of America

978-1-942557-62-3

Acknowledgments

There are not adequate words to express my deep gratitude to each person who has supported me during my first thirty years of life.

To my parents who love me enough to hold me to a high standard: thank you.

To my brother who would not let me quit: thank you.

To my entire family, who treats me as an equal part of the family: thank you.

To my friends who supported me during those years when I was adjusting to life without sight: thank you.

To my closest friends, who continually value me as a whole person: thank you.

To my mentors, who teach me how to reach my greatest potential: thank you.

And to Jira, my first guide dog, who literally showed me that I could move forward in life as I harnessed courage: thank you!

Contents

Introduction

As a nine-year-old I was faced with the reality that I had been diagnosed with an eye disease. My family and I were told that I would eventually become blind. However, the rate that my vision would decrease was unknown. Over the next ten years I experienced the traumatic transition of adjusting to life without sight.

In this account I share the incredible journey of the first thirty years of my life. This journey has been difficult, frustrating, and overwhelming, and yet also one I have sought to live with courage, joy, and love. My goal is that each page of this book shares the different ways I have experienced grit and gratitude in the face of adversity.

I write in the hope that each person will be able to apply grit and experience gratitude regardless of the situation he or she is experiencing. It is my deep desire that the lessons I have learned from overcoming major obstacles can help empower and equip people to overcome the deepest challenges they face.

Chapter 1

Loving Life as a Child

Picture the child who is outgoing and confident. The well-adjusted child who is good at home, school, and everywhere. Well, that was me. Growing up in Greenville, South Carolina, a small southern town, I was that child. I never met a stranger, and I was always outgoing, even as a toddler. In fact, my family tells the story that I was the leader at my three-year-old dance recital!

For a year, my three-year-old dance class worked hard on learning a dance for this recital. We knew the dance and were ready to go. On the day of the recital, we were all dressed in our pink leotards, pink tutus, and ballet shoes. We walked out on stage to perform the best dance of our lives! Well, as the music started, everyone in the class froze—except for me! I remembered every step. So I started motioning for the other three-year-olds to follow, and we successfully completed the dance for all our parents and everyone else attending the show.

As a young child, I was fearless at the dance recital and I was fearless at home. Having a brother who was five years older, I quickly learned how to climb trees, build forts, and ride as fast as I could down the street on my bike. No hands, of course! I wanted nothing more than to keep up with my brother and his friends. So, climbing to the top of the huge magnolia tree in our backyard was perfectly normal! My brother taught me to be tough, and I learned the value of being the baby of the family. You know how it goes with siblings. My brother and I would start arguing about something and as soon as one of our parents came in the room, I was the first to say, "He started it!" Of course, I would say that I got in trouble more than my brother did, but the reality is that I mastered the art of getting out of trouble most of the time at home.

I was not only fearless, tough, and outspoken at extracurricular activities and at home, I was also the child who behaved well at school. I would play with any of the children who did not have a friend. I remember in kindergarten playing on the playground and noticing there was a girl from my class who was swinging alone. No one was playing with her. So I decided to go and swing with Sarah. At recess for the rest of the year, I would swing with Sarah on the playground. And I was always a good student for my teachers. I never gave the teachers any problems; I always did what was right. I helped the teachers clean up the classroom and keep everything just perfect. In fact, I received the citizenship award in first grade for having good behavior in the classroom.

Life as a first-grader went great! The first seven years of my life was full of family, friends, and fun. Growing up with a mom who was a teacher was wonderful because I got to play school every day at home with her old lesson plans and classroom rolls. Each summer I loved spending time in her classroom. As she spent time getting her five-year-old kindergarten room ready for the school year, I was busy teaching my own class in her room! I loved nothing more than being in her classroom and pretending I was teaching a classroom of five-year-old kindergartners for the day. I would start the day by calling the class roll. Then I would have the pretend students sit in a circle and we would sing songs. After I led the class through the morning music we would have center time, where the pretend students played in the house center, the block center, the math center, and the reading center. Life as a schoolteacher was great! As I enjoyed being a teacher like my mom, I also thought I was such a grown-up when I got to go places with my dad. As a real estate broker he would often travel to check on different properties, and I enjoyed going along. We would pull up at one of the pieces of land and I would jump out of his white truck as if I had been in real estate for years! Once out of the truck, I would check on the sale sign or whip out a measuring tape and start stepping off the land. Pretending I was a confident Realtor was just as much fun as being a pretend schoolteacher.

Childhood also was filled with the joy of being a little sister. I thought the purpose of life was to annoy my big brother—as well as idolize his every move. I could teach a course on ways to drive your brother crazy! For example, Rob would be sitting at our dining room table working on his first-grade math assignment and I would not leave him alone. As a two-year-old, I would not stop talking. I know that is a shock! So when Rob had all he could take of his sister pulling up on the dining room table, he threw down his pencil, looked down at me with all of his frustration, and said, "Laura you are weird!" Without missing a beat, I looked up at him proudly and said, "I not weird. I LaLa." Enough said! My confident two-year-old self knew my name and I was claiming it! These days, I don't allow my family and friends to comment on the "Laura, you are weird" statement because, well, they just might agree that Rob was completely right!

Regardless, I was a happy child who loved to talk, nonstop, and be with my big brother. Even though Rob called me weird, that didn't stop me from being a mischievous younger sister. The morning arrived when Rob was ready to start third grade. Getting ready for school that morning went as planned. Rob left for school in his new clothes and was excited to be back with friends. The school day started and the teacher asked the children to pull out a notebook. Rob proudly reached down and began unzipping his brand new backpack. As soon as he had it open, Rob reached in to grab his notebook and, much to his surprise, he pulled out a bright yellow banana peel! Yes, his three-year-old sister thought it would be a great idea to send Rob off to school for the first day of third grade with a nice little banana peel! Needless to say, he was so embarrassed, and I heard all about it once he got home.

> REGARDLESS, I WAS A HAPPY CHILD WHO LOVED TO TALK, NONSTOP, AND BE WITH MY BIG BROTHER. EVEN THOUGH ROB CALLED ME WEIRD, THAT DIDN'T STOP ME FROM BEING A MISCHIEVOUS YOUNGER SISTER.

As much as I loved driving Rob crazy, I idolized him. I wanted to play outside with him and his friends and do everything he did. For example, if we were at the pool in the summer and Rob jumped off the diving board, well, of course, I had to jump off too. When Rob and the neighborhood boys were in our front yard playing baseball, I was right there playing with them. Even though Rob was much bigger than me, I always thought I could win a wrestling match against him. Of course, I never did, but that did not stop me from trying day after day.

In addition to my parents and brother, I grew up close to both grandmothers and a large extended family. Unfortunately, I did not have the opportunity to know my grandfathers because one died before I was born and the other died when I was just five weeks old.

My paternal grandmother lived across the street, so I was always at her house. As a young child, as I started elementary school, I would spend every afternoon at her house. Each afternoon I would run up the steps to her front door, fling open that door as wide as it would go, and scream "Mama B, it is me!" As if she had no clue who it was! I went straight to the kitchen table, where my snack was waiting. Some days it was strawberry ice cream, other days it was macaroni and cheese, and my all-time favorite was baked apples. After I inhaled my treat, I would go to the den, plop down on the couch, and enjoy an afternoon of TV game shows. During commercials, or after the game shows were over, I would walk across the den to Mama B's record collection and pick out a record to play on her record player. Sometimes between the snack, games shows, and record playing, Mama B would pull out a bag of marbles, and we would play. I can still see the bright colors of each marble and feel the excitement of rolling the marbles across her living room floor.

As I spent time at Mama B's house, I also spent time with her delivering Meals on Wheels. My grandmother was passionate about spending her time serving at Meals on Wheels. The program is a nonprofit organization that prepares meals and delivers them to people who are homebound. Each Friday for more than thirty years my grandmother and one of her friends would meet at the Meals on Wheels location, load the meals into one of their cars, and deliver each one. So, as a child, I would often go with her on Fridays. I can still *feel* the excitement of delivering the meals. We would pull up at some-one's house and I would reach over to the box of meals next to me and grab one. I jumped out of the car and ran to the person's front door. I rang the doorbell and yelled, "Meals on Wheels!" with all confidence and authority, as if I had been delivering these meals for years! I do not remember Mama B ever sitting me down and talking about giving back to my community. However, I learned invaluable lessons about serving the community through her actions.

I DO NOT REMEMBER MAMA B EVER SITTING ME DOWN AND TALKING ABOUT GIVING BACK TO MY COMMUNITY. HOWEVER, I LEARNED INVALUABLE LESSONS ABOUT SERVING THE COMMUNITY THROUGH HER ACTIONS.

My paternal grandmother was a huge part of my life, but I also spent time with my maternal grandmother. Mimi lived about 15 minutes away, so I saw her each week. Through most of elementary school my brother, cousin, and I would spend every Friday night at her house. Every Friday afternoon my mom would meet Mimi to drop us off. Rob and I would jump in the backseat of her car, ready for the weekend to start. Once our cousin was with us, Mimi let us choose where we wanted to go eat dinner. Of course, three children rarely could agree on the same place! So what would Mimi do? How would she solve this dinner problem? Easy! She would go to the drive-through at each place we wanted. Usually that meant two stops. However, if she needed to go to three places, that is what she would do. Once the dinner problem was solved, we would go to her house and eat dinner at her kitchen table. After dinner we would play with the other children in the neighborhood or just play outside. When we could not be outside, we would build a huge fort in Mimi's den. All the blankets and pillows in her house made a great fort. There was only one problem. Mimi would come to the doorway between the kitchen and the den, look at each of us, and say, "Now how am I going to get to the rest of the house?" Oh, our expert fort-planning had not allowed for that potential problem! Regardless of these varying rituals, we ended every Friday night by watching the TV shows that were part of a "TGIF" Friday-night lineup, all while enjoying a homemade chocolate milkshake. Yes, made by Mimi.

When I was preschool age, Mimi would read to me each Friday night before we went to bed. I would choose a book from the white wicker basket beside her chair and then crawl into her lap. She would read the book, then tell me about the other children she read to. She would tell me about the time she spent volunteering at an afterschool program. Similar to my other grandmother, I do not ever remember her talking to me about serving in the community. However, I do remember her telling me about the time that she spent reading to children in the community. I also remember her saying to me, time and time again, "Laura, treat all people equally. No one is better or worse than another person."

After a good night's rest, my brother, cousin, and I started our Saturday morning with fresh homemade buttermilk biscuits. I would wake to the wonderful smell of warm biscuits. So I would immediately hop out of bed, run down the hall through the den, and charge into the kitchen. As I turned the corner by the refrigerator, there Mimi stood in her flowered housecoat, white bedroom shoes, and a head full of pink sponge rollers! She would already have our plates set at the kitchen table. I can still taste the warm buttermilk biscuits drizzled in honey, and still whiff the aroma of her fresh coffee brewing. Once we all ate plenty of biscuits, we would watch Saturday cartoons until our parents came to get us sometime in the late morning.

Just as my childhood was full of time with grandmothers, it was also full of time spent with extended family. The holidays and summers were not complete without trips to visit my cousins. Each holiday my parents, brother, and I would drive an hour and a half to my cousin's house, where we could play on the farm. I remember pulling up to Aunt Mary's house and jumping out to see the beautiful horses that were practically touching our car. After I checked out the house, I would walk through the pastureland checking on all the cows. As I made my way back to the house, I would take a tour through the garden to see what seasonal fruits and vegetables were growing. While all the children were outside our parents were inside preparing the typical holiday southern meal, which included a deep fried turkey, baked ham, brown rice, gravy, macaroni and cheese, green beans, creamed style corn, sweet potatoes, baked apples, and pans of homemade biscuits. Of course, I had to leave room for the homemade desserts, where I had my choice of banana pudding, blackberry cobbler, cheesecake, pumpkin pie, and sweet potato pie. Needless to say, no one left hungry! Our stomachs were full and our hearts were overflowing with the gift of family.

I spent time with my cousins during the holidays, and I would also go over to stay with them for a few days during the summer. I would stay with my cousin, who was my age, and her brother, who was a few years younger. Then, just down the street lived two more cousins who were our age. So the days were spent with the five of us playing together. Some days we loaded up and went to a theme park. Now that was fun! Spending all day riding roller coasters and cooling off with a cherry icee was a great way to spend the summer. While I spent time with my cousins on their farm, I also spent time with other cousins at the beach. Most years our family vacations to the South Carolina coast included four of my cousins and their parents. We would spend our days at the beach building sand castles, burying each other in the sand, and playing in the ocean. Mornings were spent at the beach and the afternoons swimming in the pool. If we were not at the beach or the pool, we were fishing in my family's boat.

MORNINGS WERE SPENT AT THE BEACH AND THE AFTERNOONS SWIMMING IN THE POOL. IF WE WERE NOT AT THE BEACH OR THE POOL, WE WERE FISHING IN MY FAMILY'S BOAT.

Whether I was pretending to work in the profession of my parents, annoying or idolizing my brother, spending afternoons or nights with my grandmothers, hanging out with cousins, or spending time at the beach with extended family, life as a child was filled with the unconditional love of family. It was a wonderful childhood.

It was also a life surrounded by friends. The neighborhood I grew up in was made of several streets with houses built in the 1940s. The neighborhood was filled with children of all ages. At one point there were sixty children on my street alone! Needless to say, there was always someone to play with outside or someone to have over at my house. Since our house was in the middle of the street, it was easy to put together a basketball game, a group for riding bikes, a group to play in the creek, or a group to play school.

One of my best friends lived down the street. What could be better than that? We would walk back and forth to each other's house as much as we wanted. We spent as much time together as possible. You could find us outside playing on Mary's swing set, playing basketball in her driveway, or inside playing with her Barbie house. No, I was not a huge fan of

Barbie dolls, but I was mesmerized by Mary's Barbie house! It was a girl's dream house. It was bright pink with three levels. Not only did it have a den, kitchen, and bedrooms, it had an elevator! I could spend hours sitting in front of that Barbie doll house pulling the strings that moved the plastic elevator up and down. There is no telling how many times Ken and Barbie rode that elevator up and then back down while I was there! As if the Barbie house was not enough, it was complete with Ken and Barbie's motor home. So Ken and Barbie went on many trips with me as the driver.

When the weather was nice, Mary and I would set up a lemonade stand in front of my house. I had a plastic table that was just perfect for a lemonade stand. It was bright yellow on top with a red bench on one side and blue bench on the other. My dad would carry the table outside while Mary and I proudly walked outside with our pitcher of lemonade and our money box. In no time we were open and ready for business, charging our 25 cents per cup. Our day was made when someone would give us more money and tell us to keep the change! I remember one day when Mary had the job of pouring the lemonade and being at the table, and I was in charge of going back and forth to the cars delivering the lemonade and collecting money. A neighbor pulled up in his car and said he would like one cup of lemonade. I ran back to the table to get the cup. After delivering it, I said, "That will be 25 cents, sir." He handed me a dollar and said to keep the change. I was so excited I didn't know what to do. I ran back to Mary waving the money and screaming, "We have one dollar!"

Once Mary and I were too old for lemonade stands, we would ride our bikes to TCBY and enjoy a refreshing yogurt. Chocolate mousse with crushed Oreos on top was my favorite! What an afternoon; we would then ride back to our neighborhood to join the others in play.

I was also around friends at church. Growing up in a large church gave me the opportunity to be around friends during the times we were at Sunday school, worship, Wednesday night dinner, or other church activities. I remember one Wednesday night when a group of us decided it would be fun to explore the church and run from room to room. Did our parents allow this? Absolutely not! Did we get away with it? Absolutely! . . . that is, until they caught us, and then we were in trouble.

I had lots of friends at church since I played basketball and T-ball. As early as I can remember, I was on a basketball team during the winter and a T-ball team in the spring. By no means was I the best player on the team. But I loved every minute of it. I loved cheering on my teammates—I enjoyed that more than I loved playing! But let me be honest. The best part was the lunch at a restaurant after each game! Often Mary and I were on the same team, so we would practice together before games. Then, after games, we would go home and analyze the game play by play. We would go back through the game, talking about how each player performed and how each of us could improve for the next game. You would have thought Mary and I were experts on basketball just by our conversations!

In T-ball, I was more worried about my appearance than my performance. One year our team name was the Peaches. I can still see the light orange jerseys with white numbers. I was quite concerned with how my blonde ponytail looked coming out the back of my hat. I remember one game being played in the middle of the day. I was in the outfield, squinting because of the bright sun. Was I worried about missing a ball? Not at all! I desperately wanted my sunglasses so I could stop squinting and just look pretty!

In addition to church basketball and T-ball, I also had ballet classes each week. From the time I could walk, I was part of a dance class. I vividly remember my mom driving me and my friend to class each week. My friend and I would hop out of my mom's car in our light pink leotards and white ballet skirts and run in the studio's front door. If we were a few minutes early we would sit outside the door to our dance room, waiting for the older girls to come out of class. I would stare at them as the door opened and they filed out. I thought they were the greatest things in the world, and I wanted to be just like them. Once in the room I would open my ballet bag, which was bright pink with white ballet shoes on the front and a light pink shoulder strap, take off my shoes, and put on my ballet shoes. With my leotard, skirt, ballet shoes, and hair up in a ponytail, I was ready to go! I was prepared and ready to sachet, plié, and anything else the teacher taught us. Once class was over, I would carefully take off my ballet shoes and put back on my regular shoes. My friend's mom always picked us up and took us to the convenience store down the street to get a snack. I would stand in front of the candy aisle in my pink leotard, looking at all the candy and agonizing over which I should choose. Was I in a Skittles mood? More like a Hershey bar? Maybe some M&Ms? Perhaps a Butterfinger? After much consideration, most of the time I would settle on a Ring Pop. We would talk all the way home while enjoying our snack. My friend's mom would hear every detail of dance class. When we would pull up to my house, my friend and I decided we could stay together longer if her mom forgot I was in the car! So, without fail, each time we would hide behind the van's back seat and hope she would forget us. Well, I am sad to report that this bright idea never worked!

Of all the wonderful memories, the part I loved most was the time spent on trips. I mentioned being at the beach with my cousins. Well, our annual beach trips were absolutely at the top of my list of childhood memories. Each February or March I could not wait for my parents to tell me that our plans were confirmed for our June beach trip. As a child, June seemed like years away. But I was so excited and would think about it every day. I am not sure which I loved more, the actual beach trip or preparing for the vacation. About a week before each trip I would go to a wholesale grocery store with my parents to buy all of the snacks, drinks, and candy we would need. I still remember walking into the huge store, getting an empty cart, and going up and down each aisle. By the end, our cart was full of cases of water, drinks of all kinds, bags of chips, Goldfish, and crackers. Oh, and a box of two dozen full-sized Zero bars! The beach was not complete without those Zero bars. The afternoon before we left for the beach my grandmother would show up at our house with a warm pound cake that she had just taken out of the oven. Most of the time it was the third or fourth pound cake she had made that day because the first few cakes just did not come out perfect. She could not give us an uneven pound cake! On top of the pound cake container would sit a jar of vanilla frosting. Needless to say, I was ready for the beach after the drinks, snacks, candy, and pound cake had been packed.

Each year we stayed at the same condo. So once we had made the four-hour trip to the beach, I would walk into the condo like I owned it, saying, "Oh, it is so great to be back in my condo!" My parents would quickly remind me that I did not own the place, but I wasn't listening. I was excited beyond words. A typical day consisted of waking up early to eat breakfast and then heading to the beach. Then we would come in for lunch and spend the afternoon on the water in our small fishing boat. The South Carolina coast in June is usually very hot, with temperatures in the high nineties, and a heat index of more than one hundred degrees. Sitting on the dark green benches of our boat was hot to say the least! But I didn't care;

life was perfect when I was on the water crabbing or fishing. I even tried a few times to play pretend school. Remember I was good at annoying my brother? Well, pulling out a black roll book was a great way to accomplish that goal! I remember announcing that I was going to call the class roll to see who was present. Well, I only got through about six names when I realized I might just be used as bait on the end of my brother's fishing rod if I didn't stop taking attendance! I quickly put my roll book away.

One day after a long, hot afternoon of fishing we docked at the marina, everyone got out of the boat, and we started to unload the life jackets, fishing rods, cooler, and everything else we had onboard. I'm not sure if my five-year-old self suggested the idea or if someone else in my family came up with it, but someone decided it would be a great idea to use *me* to carry all of our things back to my dad's truck. So there I stood on the dock with a bright blue shirt, purple shorts, white tennis shoes, and the entire process began. I first put on my bright yellow life jacket. Then the other three life jackets were piled on top of that one. In one hand I carried the paddle and fishing net, in my other hand I carried the three fishing rods, and off we went. I walked down the dock, up the ramp to the pier, down the long pier, and right to my dad's truck. All the while my blonde curls were flying in the breeze. I was so proud of myself! I mean, I had successfully carried everything from the boat to the truck! Now it was time to celebrate with a Coke and Zero bar! As I think back on that experience, I still remember how proud and excited I was walking down the pier covered in all of our life jackets and fishing rods. My parents still talk about the hilarious experience, and we still have the picture to laugh about and smile at the memory.

Each summer was defined by our beach trip and each fall consisted of football weekends. While time at the South Carolina coast created some of my best childhood memories, football Saturdays were right there at the top as well. My family had season tickets to University of Tennessee games. Similar to learning in February or March that the beach plans had been confirmed, getting the large envelope in the mail in August with the season tickets— that was as good as life got. For each home game, we would pack the car and drive three hours to Knoxville, Tennessee. Once we were parked I would jump out of the car wearing either a short-sleeve Tennessee T-shirt or a Tennessee sweatshirt, depending on the weather. I always had my hair in a ponytail with a Tennessee ribbon, my blue jeans, and tennis shoes. I was ready for the day! Depending on the time of the game, we would go to our friends' motor home and visit, or we would head straight to the stadium. We would go to the store beside the school store and load up on bottled water, crackers, and some type of candy. Once in the stadium we would go to our seats early to watch all the warmups. Now let me be clear about being early. We were in our seats ready to go as the kickers came on the field to warm up, which was about an hour and a half before the game! As a child, I loved it because our seats were near the cheerleaders. So I was more than happy to sit in my seat and watch the cheerleaders. As the game started, and throughout the game, I would cheer loudly and proudly as if I was one of those girls! If I was at a home game cheering with a hundred thousand other fans, or if the game was away and I was at home in my living room cheering in front of the TV, I was happy.

The first eight years of my life were so carefree. I was surrounded by a loving family and great community. While I knew that all children did not have the life that I lived, I never gave one thought to the possibility that life was about to change forever. I was a fearless and confident child. I never met a stranger and I never stopped talking. If you don't believe me, ask my family! They will tell you the only time I was quiet was when I was in the bed asleep! Life was good—and I had no idea that it would, or even could, change. You know those times in our lives that are going well. Life is normal and we take it all for granted. We are oblivious to the reality of things, to the fact that life can change in a split-second.

Those stories that we hear about family members getting sick, someone we love suddenly dying, someone losing a job, or other tragic life events? Well, those stories and those people are not just events on the news. Unfortunately, those terrifying stories affect our lives deeply as well. Eventually. At some point. We each have our own stories of normal life abruptly changing to tragic circumstances.

The unexpected life changes are like the current flowing down a river with force and strength. Then, out of nowhere, the river bends. So the current has to adjust and turn to adapt to the change.

After life is normal, and then tragedy strikes, how will we respond? How would I receive the news that my life as a normal eight-year-old is about to change drastically?

THE UNEXPECTED LIFE CHANGES ARE LIKE THE CURRENT FLOWING DOWN A RIVER WITH FORCE AND STRENGTH. THEN, OUT OF NOWHERE, THE RIVER BENDS.

Chapter 2

Forever Changed

The summer months consisted of beach trips and the fall was full of football. Winter and spring were typically quiet periods of the year. In the spring of 1992, I was in second grade. I loved my teacher, and life was quite normal. But throughout the spring my parents noticed that I would start getting closer to objects to enable myself to see them better. For example, I would walk up closer to a clock to read the time. I would hold books closer to me to read each page. As a second-grader, I noticed that the teacher's writing on the board was beginning to get harder to read. One day in class the teacher asked if everyone could read the board. I was the only one who answered no.

As my parents continued to notice this problem, my mom made an appointment for me with a pediatric ophthalmologist. My dad wears glasses, so they both assumed I needed glasses as well. The night before the appointment I clearly remember sitting on the couch beside my dad while my mom explained to me that I was going to the doctor. I thought, *Oh, this will be fun! I can get a cute pair of glasses like some of the girls in my class.* The next day, Mom picked me up from my grandmother's house and we went to the doctor. As an eight-year-old, I was not worried at all. I liked the waiting room and all the books. I was sitting in a chair next to my mom reading a book when the nurse opened the door and said, "Laura Bratton, please come back." I jumped out of my chair, put up the book, and walked with my mom through the door and to the examining room. I hopped up into the big black chair. I was not excited about the nurse putting drops in my eyes so my eyes would dilate, but it was not horrible. Then I read as many letters to the doctor as I could see. He looked into my eyes with a bright light. Next the doctor pulled the light away, sat back in his chair, and said to my mom, "There is a bigger issue going on, and I am going to refer Laura to a retina specialist." I remember wondering what the problem could possibly be. I was not scared; it was all just very matter-of-fact. Obviously, my eight-year-old mind could not imagine or comprehend what this doctor was saying.

I returned to life as normal and finished the school year. Once we were out of school for summer break, I had my appointment with the retina specialist. I talked to my brother the night before the appointment, trying to come up with a plan of how we could work together to make the appointment go well. Here was our perfect plan. Rob was going to stand behind me as I sat in the big black chair. As the doctor pointed to the letter on the chart, Rob would quietly say the letter and then I would say it out loud! Did we try our plan? No. Was it a good idea in my eight-year-old mind? Absolutely!

The day of the appointment I still was not scared. I felt confident because I had already been to the first appointment, so I knew what to expect. I again sat in a tall black chair in the examining room and had my eyes dilated. It was at this appointment that the doctor told my parents I did in fact have an eye disease. After the appointment, I remember coming back home and saying, "Oh, I have an eye problem." Once again, I was oblivious to the magnitude of the problem or the potential vision loss I would be facing.

After going to the two different doctors in my hometown, my parents took me to a pediatric retina specialist at Emory University in Atlanta. The first appointment lasted several hours and included the dilation of my eyes, the reading of eye charts, the doctor shining a bright light into my eyes for what felt like forever, and having blood drawn. The specialist confirmed that I did have an eye disease. The cells of the retina in both eyes were deteriorating, they told my parents. I would first lose my central vision. Then, eventually, I would lose my peripheral vision as well.

Emotionally, or cognitively, I did not comprehend the dramatic shift that I was soon to experience. I was just excited to be in Atlanta because after the appointment we had lunch and made a quick trip to the mall, which was the biggest mall I had ever been to in my eight years of life! Then we stopped at Starbucks on our way out of town. You know those times in our lives when we are confronted with a new situation or event, where the circumstance is unlike anything we have ever experienced? The situation is so unfamiliar to us that we do not even know to be afraid. We do not even realize, and certainly we don't understand, the potential changes that are soon to affect our lives. That was my experience as we left the doctor's office at Emory. It was like the time my family and I left the marina in our boat to go a short distance to another marina for lunch. About halfway across the creek, a storm started to develop. The sky became dark and the clouds were heavy with rain. I had no idea that the protected creek water could become two-foot seas and that our small boat could be tossed back and forth so much. Since it was my first time being in a boat on a stormy day, I wasn't afraid. I did not know enough about the effects of a storm to be fearful. In the same way, I did not know the tremendous effects of having an eye disease and the changes that were soon to take place.

I DID NOT KNOW ENOUGH ABOUT THE EFFECTS OF A STORM TO BE FEARFUL. IN THE SAME WAY, I DID NOT KNOW THE TREMENDOUS EFFECTS OF HAVING AN EYE DISEASE AND THE CHANGES THAT WERE SOON TO TAKE PLACE.

After a summer of doctor appointments, I started school as a normal third-grader. The school year continued in quite typical fashion. I did sit in the front of the classroom and have my books in large print, but there were no major changes. I continued to take dance classes, play on a basketball team, and participate in all the other extracurricular activities. Over the next few years of third, fourth, and fifth grades, I began to have a better understanding of how my life was changing. For example, I would be the last player on my basketball team to make it to the opposite end of the court in a game. This happened not because I was the slowest person on the court but because I needed to run slower so I didn't bump into anyone else. Now, on the other hand, my ability as a forward on defense increased. How, you ask? Well, I needed to be so close to the person dribbling the ball that it came across that I was super aggressive. So maybe it seemed to the other team that I was the slowest player on the court, but I was also the most aggressive one!

Similar to basketball, I noticed that I had to put more effort into each dance class than my friends did. While I could see almost everything that the dance teacher would show us, it became more difficult to see the smaller details of each step. I knew that life was changing, and yet I still did not fully understand the complexity of the diagnosis.

As I reflect on my life between 9 and 12, those years that included the shocking reality of the diagnosis and the beginning stages of change, what comes to mind? What do I think of when I comprehend the eye disease that would change my entire life? Two words leap to mind. The first is grit. What is grit? Webster's dictionary defines grit as: "mental toughness and courage; unyielding courage in the face of hardship or danger."[1] Synonyms for grit are bravery, courage, spirit, backbone, strength of will, toughness, resolve, determination, perseverance, tenacity, and endurance. In the Ted Talk called "Keys to Success" by Dr. Angela Duckworth, she says, "Grit is perseverance and passion for longterm goals. Grit is having stamina. Grit is sticking with your future day in and day out, not just for the week, not just for the month, but for years, and working really hard to make that future a reality. Grit is living life like it's a marathon, not a sprint."[2]

I experienced grit in my parents as we received this devastating diagnosis. For example, they had the courage and perseverance needed to research all that they could about my eye disease and eye conditions in general so they would better understand the process. Each of my parents had great tenacity and strength of spirit to discover resources in our community, state, and nation that would assist me as my sight gradually decreased. For example, my parents learned about the National Library of Congress, which provides audiobooks for people with disabilities. I also experienced grit in my parents as they were determined that I would stay in the mainstream school system.

I will never forget speaking to a class of middle schoolers one year when I was home from college. Before I spoke, I was in the school office. A lady walked up to me and said, "Please tell your parents thank you for the work that they did." I looked up at her, confused; I had no clue what she was talking about. I was giving the talk in a different school district than the one in which I grew up. She added, "Because of the work that your parents did for you to keep you in regular public school, countless other children who came behind you are also able to stay in public school." I stood in the office of that school not sure how to respond. I replied with a simple "Oh, that is great!" However, it just did not seem like enough. I was excited and touched to know that the bravery my parents displayed not only benefited me, it benefited many other children we will never know or meet. Their displays of grit continued long after I completed public school. How powerful for each of us to think back over our lives and know that the determination, bravery, and courage of people around us not only touches our lives in difficulty, it touches the lives of others as well. Those same traits of grit deeply affect people that we will never know.

When I think back to my interaction with this woman in the school office that day, I cannot help but reflect: How can I, too, put my actions of courage and bravery into place so others around me can benefit? What a powerful question to ask ourselves as we navigate our way through day-to-day life.

As I reflect on the grit it took for my parents to educate themselves on blindness, I also realize the grit it took for them to continue to hold me to normal standards as a child. They were brave enough to continue to raise me just as they were raising my brother. Despite the fact I had received the diagnosis of a serious eye disease, I continued to have the same rules and expectations at home. My chores still included making my bed, keeping my room clean, loading the dishwasher, and brushing our golden retriever. If I disrespected my parents or got into a fight with my brother, I was held to the same consequences. My parents taught me through their actions that I cannot use blindness as an excuse to do less or be treated differently. While I am sure it would have seemed easier in the moment to baby me or let me off of the hook from following rules, my parents chose to live into their displays of grit. Remember that Dr. Duckworth said, "Grit is living life like it's a marathon, not a sprint." My parents showed grit as they chose to raise me in a way that focused on the marathon, not the sprint. Thinking back over the grit that each of my parents had as they raised me causes me to ask myself: *Do I live each day with courage, strength, and bravery for the long term?* Or am I so caught up in the here and now that I forget to have a spirit of perseverance for the future? These are beneficial questions for all of us.

Grit came through my parents, and grit also came through my brother. As my parents did not hold me to a lower standard, neither did Rob. You know that huge family argument that revolves around who gets to sit in the front seat of the car? Rob and I frequently argued over whose turn it was to ride up front. But as we argued, he never said, "Oh, OK, since you have this new eye disease, you can sit in the front seat." When we would get into a fight and slam doors in each others' faces, he would not close the door quietly or any less hard because my vision was worse than his. If we were outside playing basketball, I didn't get some kind of pass or free shots because of my low vision. I specifically remember one afternoon that Rob and I were fighting in our living room. As always, I was losing this wrestling match. For one split-second, I stopped, looked up at him, and said: "Give me a break!" He shot a look right back at me and said, "I'm only making you tough." Did Rob dismiss or minimize the significance of my vision problems? Absolutely not! Was Rob the first one to protect me and support me? Without a doubt! Did he change the way he interacted with me as my sibling? No! Similar to my parents, Rob had the courage to know that I would need grit for the longterm marathon. So he too did not change the standard for me. Through our normal sibling interactions of driving each other crazy and yet being each other's biggest supporter, he showed me the strength of grit. I often think back to these normal interactions with my brother and reflect: where are each of us showing grit in our relationships with others? How are we showing the courage and bravery that empowers another person to have perseverance for the marathon that we call life?

FOR ONE SPLIT-SECOND, I STOPPED, LOOKED UP AT HIM, AND SAID: "GIVE ME A BREAK!" HE SHOT A LOOK RIGHT BACK AT ME AND SAID, "I'M ONLY MAKING YOU TOUGH."

This quality of grit was also demonstrated by each of my grandmothers and my extended family. Both my grandmothers were determined and passionate to hold me in prayer each and every day. They prayed for the spirit of the living God to give me strength as I faced the future. They prayed for the creator of the world to give my parents, brother, and me endurance as we navigated each day. They were faithful to pray for my pediatric retina specialist at Emory University, as well as my teachers in school. My extended family members placed my family and me on prayer chains across the country. Even though at that point in my life I had no clue about the power of prayer, I can now reflect and know that each of those prayers gave me the perseverance I needed. My community was another source of grit. Similar to my family, people at church and in the community were faithful to pray for the God of all people to hold me during the challenging days I would face. Remember that I said my parents and brother held me to the same standard? So did my community. My basketball coaches continued to treat me as an equal player on the team.

During my fifth-grade basketball season, I did not score much. Even though I had not lost much vision at this point, my vision was blurry enough that I did not try taking many shots in the game. My team was playing one of our last regular season games. It was a cold, gray day in January and we had an away game. The gym was small, with only a few rows of bleachers on each side. As typically happened, I was in and out of the game, being the aggressive forward I was. In the fourth quarter, I was sitting on the bench when my coach called timeout. The girls on the court ran over to him and huddled around him. He was drawing up a play on his clipboard. Then he turned to me and said, "Laura, come here. You are going in." I jumped up and joined the others.

Once the coach showed me the play the buzzer sounded, and it was time for the game to resume. We all ran out on the court and took our positions. We were on defense first, which I loved, because I was great at defending! Then, to the other end of the court we ran. One of the guards, Mary, dribbled down the court and passed the ball to the center, Lauren, who then was within a foot of me; she passed the ball to me. As soon as Lauren passed me the ball, she said, "Shoot." Standing at my forward position on the right side of the goal, I turned and effortlessly took a shot. Nothing but net! The place erupted in a roar. The small gym was shaking. My parents, along with the other parents and coaches, were cheering and crying. My teammates were jumping up and down and congratulating me. While I was excited to score two points, I also looked around and wondered what the big deal was. I mean, I do this all the time at home in my driveway! It wasn't until years later that I realized the power of that moment. My coaches had the determination to make sure I had the same experience as everyone else on the team. They showed me through their actions that I mattered and that they were going to do what it took for me to score.

The first few years after my diagnosis, I did not fully understand what would lie ahead. I didn't grasp the sheer magnitude of the difficulty I would face. I did not fully comprehend that so much was about to change. I would have to adapt and change my way of living. While I did not understand, my family and community understood. My parents chose to live a life of grit so that I would be prepared for the days ahead. The determination, resolve, perseverance, and courage of my mom and dad created a strong foundation for my life ahead. The strength of character shown by Rob gave me the confidence that I would need for this marathon. The endurance of my grandmothers, extended family, and community empowered me to face the future with hope. The power and gift of grit surrounded me when I was unaware of my need for grit, as each of their actions held me in a time of transition. There are countless other stories of family and friends having courage and bravery for loved ones in the face of such obstacles. What

> I DIDN'T GRASP THE SHEER MAGNITUDE OF THE DIFFICULTY I WOULD FACE. I DID NOT FULLY COMPREHEND THAT SO MUCH WAS ABOUT TO CHANGE.

a gift when we can all reflect on our lives and notice the grit that has been displayed around us.

We all have our stories, like my parents advocating for me or my coaches drawing up a play so I could score in a game. The grit of the people around us is a bit like the foundation of a house that is being built. The courage, bravery, perseverance, and determination of people around us is like the solid foundation that is created for a new structure. Yes, the house will undergo challenges such as hurricanes, tornadoes, floods, fire, and other disasters. However, the house will be better able to withstand the challenges since it is supported by a strong, firm foundation. So, too, are our lives like that house. We will most certainly experience difficulty and obstacles that are large and small. Thus, having the grit of others around us is invaluable. Taking the time to stop and become aware of those who supported us when we did not know how to support ourselves is empowering beyond words. Thinking about the grit of our past fills each of our lives with grit for the present moments and the future ahead.

When I consider the initial diagnosis that my sight was deteriorating, and the next few years ahead of me, the first word that comes to mind is grit. The second is gratitude. Webster's defines gratitude as a feeling of appreciation or thanks and the state of being grateful. Synonyms include grateful, thankful, and appreciative. Gratitude is acknowledging that there are good things in the world, good gifts that we have received. Gratitude is also knowing that the goodness is bigger than us. It is knowing that the gifts come from outside of our lives.

Brother David Steindl-Rast, who created www.gratefulness.org, explains the value of gratefulness in his TED Talk, "Want to Be Happy? Be Grateful." He says: "Now, we can ask, what do we really mean by gratefulness? And how does it work? I appeal to your own experience. We all know from experience how it goes. We experience something that's valuable to us. Something is given to us that's valuable to us. And it's really given. These two things have to come together. It has to be something valuable, and it's a real gift. You haven't bought it. You haven't earned it. You haven't traded it in. You haven't worked for it. It's just given to you."[3]

As I think back on the first few years of my eye diagnosis, there are countless people and situations for which I express great gratitude. I am deeply grateful for Peter, a little boy in my mom's five-year-old kindergarten class. Peter joined the class about halfway through the school year; my mom and her class were well into their regular routine when Peter entered. Peter was a precious little boy who was short in stature. He had dark brown eyes and dark hair. He wore thick black glasses. While Peter was not totally blind, he was visually impaired. So a vision teacher came to my mom's classroom to educate her on the accommodations she would need to make in her room. Once Peter joined the class, Mrs. Matthews came three times a week to work with Peter and help my mom with any accommodations. Everything went great. Peter jumped right into the flow of the class and the school year finished well. I met Peter a few times and got to know him and his siblings. Now, why do I have so much gratitude for Peter? Why is Peter the first example of gratitude that I chose to share here? One word: timing! Peter joined my mom's class the winter before I was diagnosed with an eye disease the following summer. Peter was part of my mom's class the school year before I started having eye problems. When Mrs. Matthews walked in my mom's classroom, my mom never dreamed her own daughter would begin working with Mrs. Matthews two years later to learn braille. When I was playing with Peter and his siblings, I had no clue that I, too, would be visually impaired just like him. I tell this story because I am grateful beyond words that

Peter came into our lives a year before I was diagnosed. I am thankful for all that my mom learned about making accommodations for a visually impaired student in the classroom, because a year later she was able to take those same principles and apply them to her daughter's life at home. What deep gratitude I have for those events in our lives that help us navigate through adversity! Even though the events occur before the adversity begins, the events give us the tools we need to move through the challenge. Think about your own life. What people or events have prepared you to overcome and have courage in the face of difficulty?

> EVEN THOUGH THE EVENTS OCCUR BEFORE THE ADVERSITY BEGINS, THE EVENTS GIVE US THE TOOLS WE NEED TO MOVE THROUGH THE CHALLENGE.

I also have deep gratitude for Mary. As I shared, Mary lived close to me and we spent so much time together. When I was in fifth grade, Mary came over on my birthday. She walked in my front door, handed me my present, and begged me to open it! We sat down on the burgundy couch in my living room while I opened the gift. I quickly tore off the wrapping paper, and there was a purple basket with a blue handle. The basket was full of goodies. I honestly do not remember most of the gifts in the basket—except for one thing. The largest gift in the basket, the gift that was sticking out the top, was a dark blue ruler. I pulled out the ruler to find that it was a large print ruler. Not only was it dark blue, Mary had taken a black marker and written each of the numbers in black. Mary knew that I could see just fine if there was a contrast between colors. So if the print was white and the background black, or vice versa, I could read just fine. Mary knew that I would need a ruler for the start of the school year.

So she created a ruler that I could use. I have received many gifts through life. I cannot remember most of them. However, I will never forget that large print ruler that was dark blue with black numbers. As I received and used the gift I was thankful to Mary on a practical level. I was thankful I had a ruler I could use in school. Over the years, as I have thought back and remembered that ruler, I am thankful on a much deeper level. I am filled with gratitude that Mary cared enough about me to give me a gift that met my needs. While most fifth-grade girls would love to receive lip balm, nail polish, clothes, jewelry, or any other fun accessory, there was nothing better that I could have received from Mary. (Now, don't get me wrong. I loved my lip gloss, and I couldn't get enough of it!) But with the circumstances of my life, Mary's gift conveyed to me that I mattered. She was saying, "I know you will need a ruler like every other student in class, so here is the ruler that is accessible for you." If Mary had not given me the ruler would I have gone without an accessible ruler? Not a chance! Was receiving the ruler from Mary more powerful? Absolutely! Through the ruler, I learned the value of taking the time to think about the gifts we receive. The gifts that meet us right where we are, those gifts that make our day-to-day life a little bit easier. The gifts are not always flashy and fun, but they touch our spirits on a deep level.

I am so thankful for my parents. Both my mom and dad had the grit to hold me to a high standard, and for this I am deeply grateful. Through their actions I learned that I cannot use blindness as an

BOTH MY MOM AND DAD HAD THE GRIT TO HOLD ME TO A HIGH STANDARD, AND FOR THIS I AM DEEPLY GRATEFUL. THROUGH THEIR ACTIONS I LEARNED THAT I CANNOT USE BLINDNESS AS AN EXCUSE.

excuse. My parents continued to expect me to make my bed, clean my room, load the dishwasher, and brush our golden retriever, Shelby, and these things taught me much more than just doing chores. Continuing to do daily tasks around the house taught me that I could contribute and be an equal part of the family. I learned through my parents' actions that I was not going to be a victim to this eye disease at home, school— or anywhere in life.

My parents also made sure I continued to be part of many fun activities. For example, I could have stayed home with a family member for football games. Rather than staying home, my parents bought me a pair of binoculars and off I went to the football games! Now, our seats were not the best in the stadium; the fourth row in the end zone is not the seat where everyone wants to be. Except for one type of person! The person who is losing her sight! Our seats were perfect for me because we were so close to the field that I could see every down that was played on our end of the field. As soon as the players were on the opposite end of the field, I would whip out my binoculars and watch the game like everyone else.

One year my family and I were in Florida for a bowl game. It was the day before the game and we were driving to Orlando. All of a sudden, I began crying. No, it was more like wailing. Thinking that I was hurt or something was terribly wrong, both my parents turned quickly to determine the problem. Between tears, I stopped long enough to say, "I left my binoculars at home! I will not be able to see the game!" I had realized in that moment that I forgot to pack my binoculars, and I was devastated. My parents assured me, however, that they sell binoculars in Orlando, and that we would be able to find a pair. Later that day we stopped at a store. My parents were right; there were binoculars you could buy in Orlando! I proudly chose the right pair and walked out of the store with confidence knowing that I would now see the game like everyone else.

I am greatly appreciative that my parents taught me the powerful lesson that I cannot go through life using blindness as an excuse. Whether it was at home doing chores, at school completing work, or out having fun with family or friends, they taught me that blindness would not be a crutch that I would lean on. Rather, they showed me, we all would make the necessary accommodations so I could be an equal part of life. How easy it is for all of us to use our challenges and obstacles as excuses. Sometimes it just feels easier to stay home and feel sorry for ourselves rather than put in the effort required to make an activity accessible. Thus, I am overwhelmed with gratitude that my parents taught me early on that I cannot use my limitations as excuses.

Rob would not allow me to use blindness as a crutch either. Whether we were fighting over whose turn it was to sit in the front seat, wrestling in our den, or playing basketball in the driveway, Rob treated me like a normal sibling, and for that I am so thankful. Appreciation was about the furthest thing from my mind as I was being slammed to the floor during a fight or losing the battle to sit in the front seat of the car! However, appreciation is all I can think of now when I remember those moments of sibling rivalry. Simply, and powerfully, my brother, like my parents, taught me through his actions that I was worthy of being treated equally along with everyone else. Rob showed me in those first few years of the eye disease that I would not have pity for myself. I would not sit back and allow life to pass me by. Rather, I would move forward pursuing my goals.

One summer afternoon when it felt like 100 degrees, we were at the beach on our boat. We were anchored and had been fishing for a while. As we packed up the fishing supplies and prepared to head back to the marina, Rob fired up the motor and shouted over the noise, "Pull up the anchor." So, as an excited eleven-year-old would, I jumped on the bow of the boat and started pulling up the rope. I thought, *Yeah man, look at me go! This is easy!* But how quickly I forgot that the easiest part of pulling up the anchor is at the beginning. As you get closer and closer to the anchor, it gets more and more difficult. I pulled with all of the strength I had. I pulled that rope until I could not pull anymore. I turned back to Rob and screamed, "You come pull it up." Without missing a beat, he shouted back, "Keep going. You are close!" That was not the answer I wanted; I was hot, sweaty, and tired. My arms hurt and I could already feel the rope burn on the palms of my hands. All I wanted was for Rob to come and take over, and what did he say? "Keep going. You are close!" So that day, hot and exhausted, what did I do? I kept pulling. I pulled the rope with all that I had. I used strength I did not know was within me. At last, the anchor was right at the boat! I splashed it into the water a few times to get the mud off, and then I threw the anchor in the boat as if it had been no struggle at all. I sat back on my knees, right there on the bow of our boat, with pride at my accomplishment.

LITERALLY AND FIGURATIVELY, ROB TAUGHT ME THAT I WOULD NOT USE MY BLINDNESS AS A REASON NOT TO LIVE A FULL LIFE. HE SHOWED ME THAT WE ALL HAVE TO MOVE FORWARD REGARDLESS OF THE CHALLENGES.

Literally and figuratively, Rob taught me that I would not use my blindness as a reason not to live a full life. He showed me that we all have to move forward regardless of the challenges. Sometimes the challenges in our lives are like pulling up the anchor at first; they begin effortlessly. Other times we will scream out for someone else to come and take over the challenge because it seems impossible, and yet we will hear the words: "Keep going. You are so close. You are so close to moving through the challenge." Other times, the difficult situations will feel like getting closer to the anchor, where we must use strength that we did not know we had. For the lesson learned that hot day on the boat, as I struggled, I am grateful.

I think back to that day on the basketball court and smile. What a gift the coaches and team gave me that day. The coaches did not sit the team down and say, "OK, girls, Laura is different. You know that Laura's sight is getting worse. So we all need to be careful and gentle with her." The coach did not say, "We are feeling sorry for her, so I am going to draw up a play so she can score." No, that is not it at all. Knowing I was a member of the team who had not yet scored that year, they were going to make sure that everyone on the team scored before the season ended. For my coaches' determination, I'm grateful! For the opportunity to score those two points, I am grateful.

As I reflect on Peter being part of my mom's class, Mary giving me the ruler for my birthday, my parents holding me to the same standards as others, my brother teaching me to move forward, the support of my community, love from my grandmothers, and all the other countless actions, I realize the value of gratitude. I am thankful for the strong foundation of courage, bravery, and determination. What power gratitude can have for each of our lives! As we remember the hard, sad, and difficult events in our lives, it is important to be thankful for the actions and people who gave us strength to continue forward. Are we thankful for the challenges? Of course not! Are we deeply thankful for the people and events that helped us to move through the challenges? Absolutely!

Realizing the moments of gratitude, mixed in with the challenges and adversity, is healing beyond words.

Chapter 3

Reality Sets In

Remember your middle school days? Those years in which everyone is trying to fit in? For many of us, middle school is a difficult time. For me—as opposed to my carefree elementary school days—the three years of middle school were anything but easy and carefree.

The middle of August arrived, which meant school was starting. Vacations, time with cousins, and days at the pool were over. It was back to the school routine of getting up early and nights of homework. As the year began the necessary accommodations had been made so I could fully participate in every class and complete each assignment. The accommodations included having my textbooks in large print, worksheets and other handouts also in large print, and arrangements for me to sit at the front of each classroom. I was given a locker that was on top and at the end of a row so I could find it more easily. Everything was set and ready. Accommodations were made and my outfit for the first day of middle school had been purchased. I was nervous, but so excited! On one of the last days of summer, I vividly remember standing in my kitchen talking to Mary and telling her I was nervous about starting middle school. Mary leaned against the kitchen counter and said, "Oh, Laura, you will do great. You will do just fine finding all of your classes. Trust me, you will be able to get all of the homework finished. You have nothing to worry about!" I stood in the doorway of the kitchen thinking about what she had said. I thought, *Are you sure?* I believed Mary because she was my friend; she was assuring me I would survive sixth grade. Yet I was still nervous and apprehensive. I was anxious about keeping up with my school work as I used large print and magnifiers. I was most nervous, though, about the social aspect of middle school. Would I fit in? What would all the new students be like? Would they like me? Would my clothes be cute enough? The almost-sixth grade Laura had no idea that life was about to change, and dramatically. And in retrospect, if my only worry in sixth grade had been whether my clothes were cute enough, it would have been great!

The middle school year began as planned. Mary was right when she said I was going to do fine, even enjoy it. I found my classes without trouble, completed homework, and loved being around new students.

A few months into sixth grade, I was sitting in geography class completing a worksheet. The class was quiet as we were focused on the assignment. I leaned forward to read the directions on my large print sheet. I could not read the words as well as I had before. So I held the paper even closer to my face. As I sat there at my desk, I realized I was reading the directions much slower than I normally would because each letter looked so blurry. I stood up from my desk and walked over to my CCTV and sat down. A CCTV is a machine that magnifies print and displays it on the screen. So I was able to put print underneath a screen and the print would show up on the small screen. I could place textbooks or handouts on the CCTV and then see the print well. So this particular day in geography class, I put the handout under the screen and waited for the print to appear. Once the print was on screen, I adjusted it so it would be larger. I was struggling to get the print at the right size. The words would look too big, too blurry. Then I turned the knob on the screen so the print would be slightly smaller. With the words smaller and less blurry, I was still having trouble. I leaned up in the chair so my face was nearly touching the screen, and I tried again. With my face practically on the screen, I adjusted the knob; that made the print larger and more blurry or smaller and less blurry. I was having such a hard time. I was having to read each word letter by letter as it appeared on the screen.

After that frustrating experience, and after many other attempts at reading print in textbooks and on the board, it was clear to my parents, teachers, and me that reading print was no longer an option if I was going to keep up with the normal pace of school.

YOU KNOW THOSE TIMES IN LIFE WHEN WE HAVE TO MAKE HUGE CHANGES IN THE MIDST OF LIFE EVEN AS IT CONTINUES ON? IT'S NOT EXACTLY LIKE WE CAN PRESS THE STOP BUTTON ON LIFE.

You know those times in life when we have to make huge changes in the midst of life even as it continues on? It's not exactly like we can press the stop button on life so everything will freeze while we figure out how to work through an issue. Quite the opposite! Life continues to move at full speed, and we are struggling to adapt and move forward. If only there had been a stop button in sixth grade! Unfortunately, there wasn't. Fortunately, there were teachers, friends, and family there to help me each step of the way. I transitioned from reading text-books in large print to having the books on audiotapes so I could listen to the material. The teachers, or another student in class, would read the handouts to me. I would take the test by having the teachers read the exam, and then I would give them my answers. During the time that the other students were going to related arts classes, such as gym and art, I was working with a vision teacher. The vision teacher was working with me as I learned braille. I will never forget what a strange experience it was to learn braille. My teacher and I would sit in an empty classroom and I would practice by reading kin-dergarten-level material. I would sit there and read out loud to my teacher sentences like, "See Spot run." "Watch Sally jump." "The cat played with the dog." Then the bell would ring. My time practicing braille was over and it was time to head to algebra. I would slip the kindergarten-level braille book into my backpack and walk across the hall to algebra. The second bell would ring and I would reach into my backpack, pull out the braille algebra book, and open it to the correct page. In the span of ten minutes, I was sitting in one classroom with a teacher helping me to become proficient at braille, and then, a short time later, I was sitting in algebra class struggling to read algebra in braille. I could have used a stop button at that time!

I continued through middle school in an awkward dance of learning braille while also using braille in class. Teachers, and my closest friends, also continued reading material to me at school. While at home I would listen to my textbooks in audio format and have my mom read homework to me so I could complete each assignment.

As my vision deteriorated and I was no longer able to read print, my parents, teachers, friends, and I worked to make the necessary accommodations so I could continue in school. As accommodations for each class were made, there was another level of adjustments. I quickly realized that losing my sight meant I was different from other students. Suddenly I went from being a normal middle school girl to being different. I went from blending in to being called the blind girl. One day when the final bell rang I was standing outside with one of my best friends, Emily. As two girls walked by, they got in my face and said, "You are blind." As they ran away I said, "I am not blind, I am low vision!" It felt like those two girls had punched me in the face, knocked me down, and trampled over me. There I was standing with Emily talking about our day, comparing how much homework we had, talking about how excited we were that we had dance class that afternoon. It was a normal conversation between two middle school girls. I was quite aware that I was losing my sight and that I was different. So when the two girls ran up to me to tell me I was blind, I was hit with reality—and judgment. Those girls named the fact and the reality that, "Yes, I am going blind. Yes, I am now different." I was not in a place, emotionally, to accept that fact. I had started the grieving process for my sight. I was drowning in what is often the first step of grief: denial. I was nowhere close to accepting the fact of my vision loss. The word blind was the worst word in the English language to me at that point. Those two girls who were outside school that day could not have said a word that would have hurt me more. I was so entirely in denial that I wanted to wipe out the word—blind—from the face of the earth. You know

> SUDDENLY I WENT FROM BEING A NORMAL MIDDLE SCHOOL GIRL TO BEING DIFFERENT. I WENT FROM BLENDING IN TO BEING CALLED THE BLIND GIRL.

those times in life where someone confronts you with your reality, and you do not want to hear it? The reality is too painful, so you want to protect yourself by denying reality. That is where I was that day. I was trying to be normal and have a typical middle school conversation with Emily when reality slapped me in the face.

The denial manifested itself in depression and anxiety through my middle school years. I was depressed and overwhelmed with frustration when I realized my friends were gaining independence and I was becoming *more* dependent. For example, the reality that I was more dependent hit me hard on one particular Friday. That Friday was my thirteenth birthday, and I had to stay after school for an Individualized Education Plan (IEP) meeting. The meeting included my vision teacher, who was teaching me how to read braille, a few of my classroom teachers, my mom, and me. The purpose was to set goals for the school year, goals like becoming more proficient with braille. Now you might be thinking that such a meeting sounds helpful and productive. Yes, it was helpful, and it was needed. However, I was not exactly sitting in that meeting thinking, *Oh, this is just what I need. I'm so thankful.* I was sitting in the meeting thinking: *This is my thirteenth birthday, and I want to be doing something fun with my friends. I do not want to be here.* I did not care about reading braille more efficiently. I sat through the meeting in my seventh-grade science classroom that Friday afternoon feeling mad, sad, and frustrated that none of my friends had to have an IEP meeting. My frustration continued to increase as my friends would complete their homework in half the time it took me, and they would not have to have help from their parents. It was taking me all afternoon and night to complete homework with the help of family. I was frustrated that friends could go to fun classes like art, music, drama, and gym while I was sitting in a

I WAS FRUSTRATED THAT FRIENDS COULD GO TO FUN CLASSES LIKE ART, MUSIC, DRAMA, AND GYM WHILE I WAS SITTING IN A ROOM READING KINDERGARTEN-LEVEL BRAILLE.

room reading kindergarten-level braille. I was frustrated and depressed over the simple actions that had become so difficult for me, actions not difficult for my friends. For example, opening the lock on my locker became impossible. Seeing the small white numbers was something I could no longer do.

And as simple tasks became harder, my anxiety increased. How would I get it all done? How would I move forward? I was anxious about my own actions and anxious about the way I would be treated by others.

As the anxiety and depression increased, I had one mantra for my life. There was one statement I said to myself over and over, day and night. Unfortunately, it wasn't a good one. It was two short words: "I can't." I would tell myself during the school day, "I can't." I would tell myself when doing homework, "I can't." I would tell myself when laying out my clothes for the next school day, "I can't." I would lie in bed trying to fall asleep, praying to God, "I can't." I would cry and scream at God as I repeated over and over, "I can't." While I was frustrated beyond words that my sight was deteriorating, and while I thought it was not fair that I was going through this horrible experience, my overwhelming and dominant thought was, *I can't.* I told myself: *I do not have the strength to live life as a blind person. I do not have the strength to adapt to all the change. I do not have the strength to do what it takes to get through middle school, not to mention high school.* I would have panic attacks. Many people know those horrible moments of anxiety that result in a panic attack. Those moments when your heart starts racing so hard it feels like it is going to beat right out of your body. As your heart races, the palms of your hands get sweaty, and your breathing gets more shallow with each breath. I would often have panic attacks at school or at night when trying to fall asleep. And the horrible anxiety was mixed with depression. There was nothing worse than lying in bed trying to fall asleep and beginning to have a panic attack, only to be so depressed I could not work through the attack.

My mom told me that she had found a counselor I could see when I was ready. And what was my response? "Oh, thank you, Mom, for doing that. Yes! I am ready and want to go see the counselor as soon as I can." Absolutely that was not it! It was just the opposite. My internal response was: I am fine. I do not need a counselor. Was I still in the denial phase of grief? Yes! Even though I would lie in bed having panic attacks and depression, I was still not ready to face the blindness and work through the emotions. It seemed easier to deal with the anxiety and depression rather than receive help to cope with the horrible feelings. It seemed easier to scream at God, saying, "I can't," rather than stopping to receive God's help.

Toward the end of eighth grade, I finally got to the point that I was ready to see a counselor. But I am not sure I was as ready to work through the emotions as I was to complete eighth grade. To accomplish that, I had to get help for my anxiety and depression. In order to get up out of bed in the morning and have the ability to focus on schoolwork, I had to accept more support.

One night I was lying in bed trying so desperately to fall asleep, as often happened. I prayed to God, "I can't. I can't." Then a panic attack started and the cycle continued. In between one of the screams, during which I was telling God that "I can't" . . . I realized that I was right. I was right that I could not do life as an anxious and depressed middle schooler. I could not live adjusting to life without sight while battling panic attacks and depression and screaming at God that "I can't." What I began to realize equally, in that moment, is that I could live life as a middle schooler who was adjusting to life without sight. I could live receiving strength from the God who created me. The strength would come each moment from my parents, brother, family, friends, teachers, community, strangers, and all of creation. Lying in bed that night, my whole perspective changed. Did I jump out of bed joyful and full of peace? Not even close! Was the deep anxiety and depression gone? Not a chance! Was I willing to now take the first step toward receiving help? Yes. My experience that night was not a magical transforming event in which life suddenly became easy. The experience that night was transforming because I gained the ability to slowly let go of the thought and prayer of "I can't" and began to believe that maybe, just maybe, there was another thought and prayer for my life.

For me, the first step of changing the "I can't" was to tell my mom I was ready to go to a counselor. So I started meeting with a therapist once a week. It was exhausting work as I talked about my fears and worries. Yet it was healing to learn how to cope when I had panic attacks and suffered from depression. Middle school continued to be frustrating and overwhelming as I balanced the school work with the range of emotions I was experiencing. So I completed middle school somewhere in the worlds between denial and acceptance. I was not in complete denial that I was losing my sight. I was more willing to receive help than before. Yet I was nowhere close to fully accepting my new reality.

The middle school years were so traumatic, years that were full of change, fears, worries, panic attacks, and depression. I have a clear understanding of what it means for family, friends, and community to support me when I could not support myself. In the moment, during those years, I had no clue about the different ways that the actions of others were holding me and carrying me through a traumatic transition.

Just as grit held me during the time of the initial diagnosis, grit was surrounding me in immeasurable ways during those middle school years.

During my seventh grade year I was gripped with anxiety at the thought of getting through the school day. Then at night I was exhausted and overwhelmed with the feeling of depression as I tackled homework. In the mornings, I would be filled with tears as I thought about facing the day. At night, I would be frustrated beyond words as I worked to complete each assignment. If I was crying, or if I was mad as I completed my schoolwork, my brother would say to me, "Laura, quitting is not an option." Each time Rob said, "Laura, quitting is not an option," he was teaching me determination. By not allowing me to quit, Rob was teaching me that giving up and throwing in the towel on the game of life was not the answer. Even though I wanted nothing more than to wave the flag of surrender, Rob was teaching me through his words that quitting is not an option. When we find ourselves facing trauma and adversity, it seems easier in the moment to give up and stop putting forth the effort that it takes to live through the circumstances. We are completely consumed and exhausted by the difficulty, and we lose our perspective. We need people around us to be the voice of reason. It takes the grit of those around us to display actions of determination when we are crushed with the adversity of life.

> IF I WAS CRYING, OR IF I WAS MAD AS I COMPLETED MY SCHOOLWORK, MY BROTHER WOULD SAY TO ME, "LAURA, QUITTING IS NOT AN OPTION."

So when my brother told me that giving up was not an option, he was providing the voice of reason I badly needed. He was giving me the grit that I could not have for myself in those moments of hopelessness. Most of the time when Rob said, "Laura, quitting is not an option," I thought, *You are wrong! You do not have a clue what I am going through and how I feel!* I was frustrated in the moment because I wanted Rob to say, "Oh, Laura, you can just stop trying. You never have to do anything the rest of your life."

I was right; Rob did not know what it was like to become blind. He did not know what it felt like to experience the intense emotions I was feeling. And yet he did not have to know what it was like to adjust to blindness or experience my emotions to tell me that quitting was not an option. Rob loved me too much to allow me to quit. He knew that my parents loved me too much to let me give up. He knew that our extended family, as well as the community, loved me too much to let me give up. Rob knew that I would not want that for myself either. Giving up was not in the DNA of our family. Rob knew I was not created to quit. So he was going to hold me accountable to moving forward even in the face of unthinkable circumstances. "Laura, quitting is not an option," were the first words out of Rob's mouth during those times when I was hopeless and overwhelmed. Rob would also say, "We are going to drop back and punt." Rob was a senior in high school and was the starting quarterback for his team,

ROB LOVED ME TOO MUCH TO ALLOW ME TO QUIT. HE KNEW THAT MY PARENTS LOVED ME TOO MUCH TO LET ME GIVE UP. HE KNEW THAT OUR EXTENDED FAMILY, AS WELL AS THE COMMUNITY, LOVED ME TOO MUCH TO LET ME GIVE UP.

so most of the analogies and life lessons that I learned came through football terms. So what did Rob mean by saying we would drop back and punt? What in the world did that have to do with my declining sight? One word: perseverance.

Each Friday night as Rob quarterbacked his team, he would lead the offense through a series of plays as they drove the ball down the field. Sometimes the plays would be executed perfectly and Rob and the offense would move down the field, quickly scoring touchdowns. Other times it was much harder and required much more effort and time to score a touchdown. Then sometimes the offense he led could not move the ball no matter what play was called. Rob would line up at quarterback, call the play, and the offense would not gain a yard. Again the offense would line up for second down: zero gain. On third down, the team lined up, and this time they not only did not gain a yard, they lost yards. So what did they do? As quarterback, did Rob gather the team together and say, "OK, we are ending this game"? Of course not. They dropped back and punted! The punter came on the field, kicked the ball to the other team, and Rob's team went on defense. Meanwhile, Rob huddled around his coaches and teammates and they discussed what happened and what plays they would run the next time the offense was on the field. Clearly, the plays that Rob and the offense were running were not working anymore, so they had to figure out plays that would move the ball again.

So when Rob told me we were going to "drop back and punt," he was telling me that the play-calling for my life was changing. The way that I had been living was not working anymore. Reading large print and using a magnifier was not possible. So, like Rob on those Friday nights when the offense could not move the ball, I would come together with my family, teachers, and community to figure out what I needed to do to complete school, work through my emotions, and move forward in life. A new plan for the game had to be figured out. It would not be easy and effortless, like those times when Rob made one long pass and the team scored a touchdown. Rather, it would be a game of perseverance, and I would have to learn a new way of living.

Whether you are obsessed with football or have zero interest in the game, the principle is the same for each of us. There are times in life when we are going through on autopilot and things are going along quite normal. Then, out of nowhere, life comes to a screeching halt. We are abruptly confronted with adversity, difficulties, or trauma. What do we do? How do we move forward? In the initial onset of the adversity and in the days that follow, it takes the perseverance of those around us, as well as from ourselves, to live each moment. Notice that my brother said, "We will drop back and punt. Laura, you will not quit. We will drop back and punt." Rob did not say, "Laura, you will not quit, and Laura, you will drop back and punt." What is the difference between the two? The difference is a game-changer! If Rob had told me to drop back and punt, he would have been saying, "You, by yourself, will persevere and move forward in the face of becoming blind." By saying, "We will drop back and punt," he was teaching me that as a family we would persevere and do whatever it took so I could live life as a person who is blind. The word *we* represents my teachers who taught me braille as well as the teachers who made the needed accommodations for me so I could be an equal part of their class. The *we* represents my parents, who are my advocates

BY SAYING, "WE WILL DROP BACK AND PUNT," HE WAS TEACHING ME THAT AS A FAMILY WE WOULD PERSEVERE AND DO WHATEVER IT TOOK SO I COULD LIVE LIFE AS A PERSON WHO IS BLIND.

and will never stop supporting me. The *we* represents Rob, who is my biggest fan and will not let me quit. The *we* represents my extended family and friends who love me—sighted or blind. The *we* represents the community who empowers me to move forward.

When adversity strikes and we are face to face with problems, difficulties, and obstacles, we are not expected to move forward with the perseverance of our own strength. Facing a traumatic situation square on can leave us feeling isolated. We instantly feel alone, as if there is not a person on the face of the planet who can understand. Not one breathing soul can possibly know what we are going through. In the initial days of my traumatic transition to losing my sight, I was the queen of putting my hands on my hips, stomping around, and saying, "No one gets me. No one understands." And if I am honest, I have to say that I still have those moments when I am convinced no one understands.

While we experience these feelings of isolation, it is vital that we allow those around us to persevere for us. Even though we think our family, friends, and community cannot possibly understand our situation, we need their gift of perseverance as together we drop back and punt.

The determination and perseverance of my family, friends, teachers, and community surrounded me during those traumatic middle school years. As I become aware of the grit that held me together, I cannot help but be overwhelmed with gratitude. I am deeply grateful for the gift of Rob, who taught me through his actions how to display courage and perseverance. At the time, I thought he was being mean and unreasonable in telling me that quitting was not an option. Now I could not be more thankful that I had people in my life who cared enough about me to not allow me to quit.

* * * * * * *

Like most households with children or teenagers, the morning routine at our house was rushed and crazy as we got ready for work and school. The morning started as my mom ran with several friends before getting ready for the day. Typically, my alarm had gone off and I was struggling to get the energy to get out of bed when my mom would come back in from running. She was energized and ready for the day to begin; I was just trying to force myself out of bed and put one foot on the floor. She would come into my room and excitedly announce that she and her running buddies had been praying for me that morning. I would mumble something like, "Thank you." It was 6:30 in the morning and I was anything but thankful. I had spent most of the night battling panic attacks mixed with depression. And now it was morning. It was time yet again to face another day of school and anxiety. So hearing that my mom and her running group had been praying for me quickly got lost in my feelings of fear and worry.

Once I was out of bed, I would go through the normal routine of showering and getting ready for the day. Then I would walk up the hall from my room and turn right into the kitchen. My dad would be leaning against the counter reading the sports section of the newspaper. As I turned the corner into the kitchen, my dad would stop reading the paper, look up at me, and say, "This is the day that the Lord has made." Then, most days, he would say the second part of the verse, which is, "Rejoice and be glad in it." While opening the refrigerator and pantry, I would say, in my most teenager-ish voice, "Yeah, Yeah. I know. I know." Those words were not what I wanted to hear as I struggled to keep the panic attacks at bay. Thinking about the fears and worries of the upcoming day dominated every inch of my brain. Just as when my mom told me her running group was praying for me, I intellectually believed what my dad was saying, but in no way did I feel those things in my heart or my emotions. I was so deep in the trenches of anxiety and depression that I was nowhere close to receiving or internalizing the spiritual strength my parents were giving me.

Often in the midst of adversity we are so consumed with getting through each day that we are not able to fully receive or understand the huge impact of the gifts around us in our lives. We are too closely connected to the situation to realize the burst of strength we are receiving even in the most horrible of times. Now, years later, I can realize the huge gifts and be thankful for each of the school mornings that my mom told me her group had been praying for me, and for the moments when my dad reminded me just who was the creator of the world. What a gift that in the face of struggling through obstacles and challenges, the support around us provides strength regardless of our capacity to comprehend the benefits. I now believe and know with every fiber of my being that each prayer that my mom and her running group prayed for me gave me strength upon strength to make the necessary adjustments in school and work through the difficult emotions. I also know with everything that I have that hearing my dad say, "This is the day that the Lord has made. We will rejoice and be glad in it" also was a source of strength. During those middle school years I was usually anything but thankful for a new day. In fact, I dreaded a new day. After hearing my dad say that verse for years, however, I can now reflect and say: Indeed, that *was* the day that the Lord had made, and it was one I could indeed be thankful for. Am I thankful for the times of fear, anxiety, and depression as I went through the traumatic transition of adjusting to life without sight? I can say that I am not. So how can I reflect and know that these were the days the Lord had

made? How do I know that for me, and how do I know that
for each of our lives? I know it because we are given the gift
of God's loving spirit, a gift that sustains us even in the most
horrific times. The spirit of love comes through those around
us, those who love us deeply. They love us so much that even
in the face of adversity they will do what it takes to speak
words of support and perform actions of love. Healing gratitude comes when we are able to think back over the hardest
of times and stand at the intersecion of realizing and receiving
the spirit of love in and around our lives.

I am grateful for the support I received from my parents
and brother. I am also thankful beyond words for the support of my friends. Everyone knows how awkward and difficult middle school can be, even on the good days. The combination of meeting new students, trying to fit in, and keeping
up with schoolwork while going
through hormonal changes is a
recipe for confusion in the mind
of even the most normal middle schooler. So in the midst of
awkwardness and confusion, as
each student in my school tried
to sort out his or her own circumstances and emotions, there
was a friend whose sight was declining. My closest friends did all
they could to help me at school
as well as out of school. In classes they would read textbooks
and class handouts to me. Each afternoon Emily and I would
leave our last class a few minutes early so I could go to my
locker and get outside before the bell rang and the crazy rush
of students started. I am deeply grateful that my closest friends
responded with compassion and yet strength in continuing to

I AM DEEPLY GRATEFUL
THAT MY CLOSEST
FRIENDS RESPONDED
WITH COMPASSION
AND YET STRENGTH
IN CONTINUING TO
TREAT ME AS A NORMAL
HUMAN BEING.

treat me as a normal human being. For the help in my classes, I am grateful. For their strength to continue to treat me with respect, I am grateful. For the times in class that we acted like normal middle school girls and talked about the latest issue of *Seventeen* magazine rather than listening to the teacher, I am grateful. Was every person in middle school compassionate and accepting? Of course not. There were plenty of moments when I was ignored, stared at, and talked about because of my blindness. Were those actions performed by my closest friends? Thankfully, I can say no.

My friends were a support to me at school and out of school. I continued to stay in dance class as long as I could. For each dance class, Emily and I would take our place in the back corner of the studio. Emily could then show me any parts of the dance class I was missing. Was the dance teacher accommodating? Thankfully, she was. Was it a benefit to have Emily willing to take the time to help me when I needed it? Yes!

EATING PIZZA AND SPENDING HOURS DANCING TO MUSIC IN OUR ROOMS PRETENDING WE WERE CELEBRITIES WAS JUST WHAT I NEEDED.

I am thankful for the structured times that friends helped me in school classes, dance classes, and other situations. I am also deeply appreciative of those moments when I could be a normal middle school teenager and go to the mall with friends or take part in sleepovers or any other fun activity with friends. Now that I can reflect on that most difficult time in my life, I am grateful for the ordinary moments that gave me a taste of being a normal middle schooler. I would spend the entire week with my stomach in a knot, controlled by anxious thoughts. So to spend the night with a friend or have a friend spend the night at my house was healing to my exhausted spirit. Eating pizza and spending hours dancing to music in our rooms pretending we were celebrities was just what I needed. Did I realize in the moment that pizza combined with rap music was healing and a source of strength? I certainly did not. Once I was more removed from the situation, I could reflect and understand the healing power of normal time with friends.

One of the best times of normalcy with friends occurred at the 1997 women's college basketball Final Four National Championship game in Cincinnati, Ohio. My friend Mary, our dads, and I went to cheer on Tennessee. On the morning of the game the four of us were sitting on a couch on the second floor of the team hotel. The elevator directly to our left opened and out walked the head coach, Pat Summitt, and the players. I mean, they were only a few feet from us! Not only were they that close, I also got to speak to Coach Summitt and the players. It was a dream come true! I was so excited and nervous that I only uttered a quiet, shy hello. My life could not have been more perfect in that moment! I just spoke to the head coach and players that I completely idolized. In that moment, and for that whole trip, I was able to enjoy being a middle school girl. No, the intense reality of my situation had not changed. Thankfully, in the midst of the difficult circumstances, I was able to experience a fun trip.

All in all, those three years in middle school were anything but easy and smooth. Standing in the doorway of my kitchen talking to Mary about the start of middle school, I was nervous about the most normal of middle school worries, things like: would I fit in? Would I like my teachers? Would I have enough time between classes to get to my locker? Each of my worries quickly faded away as I was thrown into the difficult days of transitioning from print to braille and from being "normal" to being "different." I was also thrown full force into the grieving process and consumed by the intense emotions of anxiety, fear, and depression. When we find ourselves in the midst of a traumatic transition in life, gripped by difficult emotions, how do we move forward? How do we continue on when we are overwhelmed by feelings of isolation, fear, panic attack, anger, and depression? We become more dependent on the grit of our family, friends, and community. We lean heavily on the determination, perseverance, and courage of those around us. We allow those who love us and support us to carry the strength and tenacity that we are not able to carry for ourselves.

Remember that I said I was becoming more dependent and my friends were becoming more independent? While that was frustrating beyond words, it was a time of survival for me, and times like that become survival for all of us. As we battle through horrible situations in life, we survive by depending on the grit and gratitude of others. We do not survive the trauma by being independent; rather, we continue wrestling through the difficult circumstances with the love, help, and support of all creation.

Chapter 4

Struggling to Survive

The middle of August arrived and I was standing in the high school parking lot with Emily and her sister, who drove us to school. I was nervous and yet proud that I could now say I was a high schooler. I had been preparing for this day for months.

Back in the spring of my eighth grade year, I would go to the high school with my orientation and mobility instructor so I could learn the layout of the school. An orientation and mobility instructor is a teacher who is trained to teach students with any level of vision problems how to safely navigate their surroundings. Just as I worked with a vision teacher to learn braille, I also worked with this orientation and mobility instructor to learn how to use a cane and safely cross streets. For the last month or so of middle school, the teacher and I would go to the high school so I could learn the school's basic layout. I would walk the halls of the high school thinking, *Oh, wow! These halls are really wide and really long.* I was totally intimidated by the size of each hallway. As a middle school student I thought to myself, *I will never learn how to get around this school.* Now, after going to the high school once a week for four to six weeks, I was still nervous, but also much more confident. I prepared for high school by learning the layout of the school, and I also prepared for high school by meeting with the teachers I would have that fall. For example, during July, I spent time meeting with each teacher so they could learn about my needs and I could learn about the structure of their class. Many hours had been spent learning the layout of the building and preparing for each class. So now, in August, I stood there in the high school parking lot nervous to my core—and yet ready to get started.

Emily and I walked into the school and gathered with the other freshman students in the auditorium. My anxiety quickly increased, and I could not focus on the words that were being spoken to us by the assembly leaders. Once that session was over, it was the class period for me to work with a vision teacher rather than going to a related arts class. I can still vividly remember leaving the high school auditorium, turning right, walking down the hallway, which seemed forever long, turning left at another hallway, and stopping at the first door on the left, which was my vision teacher's classroom. While walking down those long hallways I stared down at the white tile, thinking that I was going to throw up at any second because I was so nervous. In middle school I was nervous about fitting in and having enough time between classes to get to my locker. Leaving the auditorium and walking down the long hallway in high school, I was anxious on a much deeper level. I was fearful and worried with questions like, "Will I survive high school?" And, "Will I be just as overwhelmed with anxiety and depression as I was in middle school?" Even though I was receiving help to work through the grieving process and getting help to work through the difficult, paralyzing emotions, I was scared that I would go back to that horrible place where I was controlled by fear, worry, panic, and depression. You know those times when we are in the midst of the adversity or trauma and start to think that the exhausting emotions are going to be a permanent way of life? We are too far into the situation to pretend all this is not occurring, and yet we are making what feels like slow progress toward healing. It is like standing on the edge of the Grand Canyon. Two short steps to the right and we could fall into the canyon, and yet two short steps to the left and we would be securely on land. Which way would high school go? Would I be thrown down into a hole of difficult emotions? Or would I stand firm on solid ground as I continued to work through the difficulties?

WOULD I BE THROWN DOWN INTO A HOLE OF DIFFICULT EMOTIONS? OR WOULD I STAND FIRM ON SOLID GROUND AS I CONTINUED TO WORK THROUGH THE DIFFICULTIES?

The questions in my head and nervousness in my stomach continued as I walked from the auditorium to the classroom. When I turned the corner and was standing in front of the classroom door, who was about seven feet from me? Mary! I had never been so happy and relieved to see my close friend standing in front of a classroom door. Mary, who was completely confident and calm, walked up to me and said, "How's it going? How is the day going so far?" Mary was a sophomore, so she had the whole high school thing figured out. As she asked me those questions, I wanted to burst out crying and scream, "Let's leave school, Mary!" But rather than having a meltdown right there in the hallway with other students and teachers walking by, I forced a quick smile, tried to take a deep breath, and said, "It is OK." Mary knew me so well she could read me like a book. She knew I was completely nervous and about to fall apart. So she gave me a quick hug and said, "You will do great today, Laura."

Middle school was spent learning braille, and my freshman year of high school was spent learning a computer software that worked as a screen reader. The screen reader audibly reads everything that is on the screen. So a person who is blind can have full access to a computer by using a screen reader. Like learning braille, learning how to use the screen reader was frustrating. While learning how to use a screen reader takes a while, the most frustrating part, once again, was the gap between what I was able to do on the computer compared to what my friends were able to do. I was sitting in a small room learning how to boot up the computer, sign on, and open a Word document. This was while other students were in another classroom creating elaborate PowerPoint presentations. It was not fair that I was sitting in a room learning how to use a computer in a completely new way while they were able to use the computer for creative projects. But while I was definitely frustrated, I was also highly motivated to learn how to use the reader. The quicker I learned to use it, the quicker I could join my friends on Instant Messenger! I would also be able to write papers and do much of my schoolwork on the computer independently rather than having someone read everything to me and then deliver the answers verbally. So I took the time required at school and home to learn the screen reader well enough that I could use the computer.

High school continued like a back-and-forth seesaw of emotions. I was working through the healing process of grief while still battling my anxiety and depression. Life was the awkward combination of becoming more aware of the true reality of my situation and yet learning how to move forward.

For example, I will never forget a conversation I had after school one day in the parking lot. I was in ninth grade and faced with the sad decision of stopping dance class. My vision was to the point that my depth perception was getting worse and I was often experiencing dizziness. Trying to dance at a higher level while having depth perception problems mixed with dizziness is quite difficult! So it had become clear that I needed to stop dancing. Could my dance teacher and I figure out a way to make it work? Of course. Could accommodations have been made? Yes. But I was at a point in which keeping up with schoolwork and working through my emotions was more than I could handle. I was not even close to having the energy needed to make dance class accessible. So one September afternoon, once school was over, I was standing in the parking lot talking to friends. I noticed that Carrie was walking over to me. She said, "Laura, I am going to dance this afternoon. Come to class." I said, "Oh, I wish I could, but I am not going to come today."

"Laura we want you there. Come! Come! Come!" she said.

I could tell in her voice that Carrie genuinely meant it and wanted me to be part of dance class. I stood there going back and forth between staring down at the asphalt and looking up at Carrie. I was filled with two intense yet opposite emotions. I was excited that Carrie missed me in dance class and cared enough about me to ask me to come back. Yet I was angry and frustrated, even beyond my comprehension, that I was being forced to stop doing what I loved. I had to stop doing the activity that I had started as soon as I could walk.

I wish I could say that working through adversity and striving to move forward in the face of difficulty was a smooth, linear process. I wish I could say it is a process in which we each feel the painful emotions and then transition to a permanent place of healing. Unfortunately, that is not the case at all! We feel hope and fear, joy and sadness, anger and peace all at the same time. Rather than emotions transferring through a linear process of feeling the negative emotions and then moving to positive emotions, we experience the entire range of feelings simultaneously. For example, I was developing healthy coping skills while still wrestling with the reality of my situation. As I continued to have weekly counseling sessions and receive the love and support of my family and friends, I slowly changed my thought patterns from *I can't* to *I can*. The nights became easier as the panic attacks decreased, and I began to feel stronger. I gained strength and confidence as I learned to do schoolwork both at school and at home more independently.

I was also filled with excitement one Friday night on the football field at about the 50-yard line. No, I did not throw or catch a long pass! Let's go back to freshman English class. It was a Friday in early October and I was sitting in the third seat up against the wall of the first row of the class. Through the school intercom one of the administrators began with the day's announcements. Not really paying attention, I thought I heard the administrator say, "On the freshman homecoming court is Laura Bratton." Then two other names were listed. I looked around, like, "Wait, wasn't that my name?" My friends in English class started clapping, cheering, and congratulating me. Friends in the class across the hall ran over to congratulate me as well. The following Sunday my mom, two of my close friends, and I shopped for my homecoming outfit. I said, "OK girls, you are going to be my personal shoppers today!" After entering many mall stores and trying on countless outfits, we found the perfect one! Black skirt with a red shirt and black jacket. (We had to have red since the school colors are red and white.) We not only found the outfit, we also found the perfect black shoes to match! Purchasing new silver earrings, necklace, and a bracelet would come later in the week.

Friday arrived, and it was homecoming. Friday afternoon we had our pep rally at the end of school. I was so excited as they called each of the names of those on the homecoming court to walk out in the gymnasium to be presented. Once the pep rally was over, I could not wait to get to my friend Maggie's house to begin getting ready. Maggie and Emily, who went shopping with me, were my hair and makeup stylists for the night. The three of us had it all planned as if we were in Hollywood! Upstairs in Maggie's room everything was so much fun. I was dressed, my hair was finished, and Emily only had a little more lipstick to add and I would be ready to go. As she grabbed the lipstick she said, "Are you nervous?" I said, "No! I am not nervous at all about winning or not. I just love going shopping, buying new clothes, and having you and Maggie do my hair and makeup."

Once at our high school stadium, my parents and I waited for Rob and his two friends to arrive. They were all football players at Clemson University. Since it worked out for them to come, we decided as a family that Rob would be my escort on the field. I told my brother's two friends that they were my bodyguards for the night! Since they were both about 6-foot-5, I considered them perfect for the job! One of the friends grew up with Rob, so I consider him to be another brother. The other friend had become a close friend of Rob's in their two years at college. So I knew both of Rob's friends well, and it meant the world to me that they came to homecoming night. We had fun laughing and joking that they would keep all of the fans away from me while I prepared for homecoming court. And then the time had finally arrived. Each of the members of the court were out on the field since it was halftime. The first winner they would announce was the freshman homecoming court. When the announcer called my name as the freshman homecoming princess, the people in the stands went crazy.

Everyone was cheering and clapping. What did I do? I froze, looked at Rob, and said, "What do I do?" He laughed and said, "You are going to start walking!" So together we walked to receive my flowers.

> I FROZE, LOOKED AT ROB, AND SAID, "WHAT DO I DO?" HE LAUGHED AND SAID, "YOU ARE GOING TO START WALKING!" SO TOGETHER WE WALKED TO RECEIVE MY FLOWERS.

Homecoming was such a fun night of being a normal high school girl. It was not about winning or losing the homecoming court. It was such a joy to think about clothes, hair, and makeup. While reality had not changed, it was healing and strengthening to take a quick break from the overwhelming and exhausting work of adapting to life without sight and to focus solely, for a time at least, on enjoying life and laughing with friends and family.

The back and forth emotions of joy and fear, peace and anger continued throughout my high school years. There were moments of fun, laughter, and joy like I experienced on homecoming night of my freshman year. There also continued to be times of intense frustration and anger. For example, I faced the unbearable reality that my friends were getting their driving permits and licenses. My close friend, Mary, was a year older than me. So when she got her license and started to drive, I thought it was wonderful because she and I could go places without our parents! The days of riding our bikes to get ice cream were over! Now Mary could drive to my house, pick me up, and we would go get ice cream or whatever we wanted. Life was great! This newfound freedom of Mary driving was fabulous. But the exciting freedom of going places with Mary quickly dissolved into intense frustration and anger as the following year rolled around. I had turned fifteen. What did age fifteen mean to a teenager in my world? Two words: driving permit. Was I studying for the driving test and nervous about passing the test? Unfortunately, no. I was living in the most difficult reality that my sight was decreasing, and I was struggling to keep up with schoolwork while working through anxiety, fear, and depression. Once again I was face to face with the reality of the limitations of being blind. The gap between my friends gaining independence and me becoming more dependent was increasing. It felt like I was suddenly forced to swim upstream, fighting hard against a current, while people my age were continuing to swim downstream with no effort at all.

I was secretly happy when my friends did not pass the written test or actual driving test. One Friday night at dinner, a friend was telling several of us that she was not able to take the written test that afternoon, as she had hoped and planned. When she arrived at the department of motor vehicles, she realized she did not have the correct documentation. So she was going to have to go back another day. The girls sitting around that restaurant table responded by saying, "Oh, that is horrible that you could not get your permit today! Sorry that you have to go back and go through that next week." But I was sitting there thinking, *Really? You are frustrated about that? At least you get to go back next week and take the test.* The frustration and anger of knowing I would never have the chance to take a written driving test was exploding in my mind. Yet, I forced a smile and continued to eat my sandwich and chips.

Throughout the year after I turned fifteen my friends, one by one, as well as other people my age, received their driving licenses. They moved into the freedom of having a car and driving whenever they wanted and wherever they wanted. During that time, I continued to work with an orientation and mobility instructor to learn how to safely cross streets as a blind person. I continued to wrestle with the gap between what my friends were now able to do and what I was able to do. Sure, I benefited from my friends being able to drive. Each friend was more than willing to take me to and from school as well as anywhere else we were going. I did not struggle with the question, "Will my friends take me places?" Instead, I struggled with intense anger and frustration that I did not have the same ability to drive.

> I CONTINUED TO WRESTLE WITH THE GAP BETWEEN WHAT MY FRIENDS WERE NOW ABLE TO DO AND WHAT I WAS ABLE TO DO.

As high school continued and I strived to learn to adapt to my new reality, I constantly felt as though I was swimming against a very strong current, and yet everyone around me was swimming along with the current. Actually, it felt worst than that. Life felt like I was swimming with the current and then, with no warning, I was suddenly swimming *against* a strong current. I was forced to swim against this current and, on top of that, the ocean waves were crashing into me. With each stroke another wave would crash and push me back so that I had to swim harder and apply still more strength. At certain times the waves seemed smaller and I seemed to be gaining ground. Yet at other times the waves were relentless and I seemed to be drowning.

How do you take one more stroke forward during those times? How do you continue to find the strength for one more breath when the salty water is stinging your face? The support, encouragement, determination, perseverance, and love of those around us is what enables us to swim against one more wave and take one more breath before the next wave crashes in. The intensity of swimming against the ocean current slowly decreases as the actions of courage and tenacity are mixed with the crashing waves.

For each of our lives the actions of courage and support manifest themselves in different ways. For my situation of adjusting to life without sight, the actions of the grit displayed by others gave me strength in different areas. As it felt like I was in the middle of the ocean swimming against the current hundreds of miles away from land or people, one of the waves I was swimming against was spirituality. I was struggling with so many passages of Scripture. While I found great comfort and strength in many Bible passages, I wrestled with many others.

One particular Sunday night I collapsed on the floor at the foot of my bed, picked up the phone, and called Martha. Martha was a family friend and we went to the same church. She had been an amazing spiritual support to my family and me during this most difficult time. Consumed by anxiety and frustration, I reached out to her. Martha answered the phone and I got right to the point of my call. I said, "I do not understand these stories and you have to explain them to me." She quickly said, "I will do my best. What stories?" With the combination of anger, frustration, and tears, I said, "Oh you know. All the stories where people are healed instantly from physical disabilities. I mean there are several stories in which Jesus heals people who are blind. So what about me? Why am I not being healed like that? I mean, I have faith in God. So why is God not healing me like the people in the stories? Martha, you and I have been praying for my healing, people at my church have been praying for my healing, my family members have been praying for my healing, people literally around the world have been praying for my healing. So why am I not like those people who were healed quickly?"

When I finally took a breath and stopped talking, I prepared myself for Martha's huge, intellectual-based answer. I just *knew* that the whole time I was presenting my argument Martha was preparing to answer my question so my tears of frustration and anger would disappear and I could rest well that night. There was a brief silence . . . and Martha tearfully said, "Laura, I do not know." With all love and support in her voice, she said, "I have those same questions. I want you to be healed like those people in the Bible, too, Laura."

Needless to say, that was not the answer I was looking for. I was hoping Martha was going to say something like, "Oh, I am glad you asked. Today at church God told me that you are going to be healed tonight. So you can go to sleep tonight and wake up tomorrow fully sighted." I wanted Martha to give me an answer that would make me just like those people in the Bible. I wanted to be healed quickly so I did not have to continue going through the extreme difficulty of adapting to life as a blind person. I wanted my sight back so I could be a normal high school girl. In the moment I was frustrated at Martha and wanted to hang up the phone. And yet Martha's words could not have been more of a source of courage and strength. Martha had the courage not to try to come up with some great answer that would make me feel better. She did not tell me to pray more or have more faith. She had the strength to jump into the ocean and swim alongside me as I struggled to make sense of my reality. She showed me through her words that I was not swimming alone against the current. She was right there giving me the ability to take one more breath

> SHE DID NOT TELL ME TO PRAY MORE OR HAVE MORE FAITH. SHE HAD THE STRENGTH TO JUMP INTO THE OCEAN AND SWIM ALONGSIDE ME AS I STRUGGLED TO MAKE SENSE OF MY REALITY.

before another wave would crash over me.

Martha's words to me on that Sunday night are an example of moments that kept me going as I wrestled with huge spiritual and emotional questions. There are countless examples of actions of perseverance that taught me how to adapt and live life as a person without sight regardless of the situation. Using binoculars no longer helped me see the field at a football game. What did my parents do? Did they say, "Oh, honey, you have to stay home and cannot go to football games anymore." Absolutely not! They bought me an AM/FM radio and off to the games we went! During this time, Rob was on the football team at Clemson University. So we were going to Clemson Tigers games as well as Tennessee games. A huge tradition at each Clemson football game is for the players to file off the bus that delivers them to the stadium, gather around a famous large rock, rub the rock, and then run down a steep hill at the stadium. Sitting in the stands, I could not see my brother, the other players that I knew, and the whole team celebrate that tradition before each game. So my parents figured out a way to adapt the situation for me. My mom and I walked around the stadium to the area where the bus arrived with the team. When the team started filing off the bus, one player at a time, I was able to see each one. Once everyone was off the bus, my mom and I would walk over to the area where the players were rubbing the rock so I could see that tradition happening as well. Since we were then standing at the top of the hill, I could see the players as they ran down the hill. Once they were on the field, my mom and I would walk back around to our seats and join my dad. I would then quickly turn on the radio so I didn't miss a play. I was frustrated and sad that I could not see my brother like the other 85,000 people in the stands and the thousands on TV. Did standing at the top of that hill take away all of my frustration and anger? It did not. But the few moments of being able to see Rob, as well as the other players, was a source of strength and joy as I continued to grieve that my deteriorating vision affected every part of my life. Through those moments of football games and other family trips, my parents and brother showed me through their actions, love, and support that together we would find ways to adapt so I could continue to live to the fullest. While life often felt like I was swimming against that current, and often left me feeling far from land—or people—these were the actions of my family, friends, and community that gave me the perseverance and determination I needed for each moment.

The moments and actions of courage that helped me adapt to life without sight also helped me display my own grit as I experienced other difficult situations. Remember that I could have used a pause button in middle school when I was trying to learn braille? Well, I could have used a pause button many times through high school as I continued to adapt to life without sight. If I'd had one, I could have adapted in that moment and not had to worry about new difficult situations happening. Unfortunately, when we are confronted with intense adversity and trauma, life continues to move forward. People around us are experiencing pain and loss as well as challenges and obstacles that, in turn, affect our lives deeply. We are not just faced with overcoming our own adversity, we are also faced with overcoming adversity and challenges from many different areas of life.

While I was continuing the grieving process of adjusting to blindness, I experienced another type of intense grieving.

It was on a Tuesday night in winter, and my mom came to pick me up from a Bible study. As soon as we got home I knew something was wrong. My dad was standing on the front porch; his face said it all. We walked inside and he told me that he had just found our fourteen-year-old golden retriever,

Shelby, dead. I collapsed in a chair while sobbing uncontrol-lably. We got Shelby when I was very young. I simply did not know life without Shelby. She was so tall that, at age three, I would literally jump on her back and expect her to run around the backyard like she was a pony! Of course, she would take off and, about three steps later, I was flying through the air and landing on the grass. I loved every minute. One of my chores around the house was to brush Shelby. I would sit on the bottom step of our deck while she sat in the grass, and I would brush her thick coat of hair, a beautiful deep red color. During those days of first experiencing my vision problems, I would sit there with Shelby as I brushed her. Shelby's deep red coat would fly all over me, her, and the backyard while we sat there in silence or, at other times, as I talked to her as I worked. On the days I was depressed and sad, I did not say a word. All I needed was to sit there brushing Shelby. I knew that she understood me and loved me even when I did not have words to speak. Other days I was anxious. I would brush her hair while talking nonstop about how scared I felt. Those moments of being with Shelby were healing beyond words. She was a source of courage. So when my dad told me she had died, I was crushed. What a huge loss it was for me because Shelby was a source of strength. I wanted her support to continue as I went through the difficult days.

Unfortunately, the death of Shelby was the beginning of a season of death for my family. A month later we received a call that my great aunt, who was like a grandmother to me, had

81

passed away. It was a Sunday afternoon in January when we got the call. Sunday night my grandmother called to tell me how sorry she was. She had already talked to my mom and dad, so she wanted to call me. I still remember the conversation like it was yesterday. She said, "Laura, I am so sorry that Aunt Mary died. I know how much you loved her and how she was like another grandmother to you." I thanked her, and for the next few minutes we talked about Aunt Mary. Then my grandmother told me that we would talk soon. So we said "I love you" and ended the call.

My grandmother had turned 80 two weeks before our phone call that Sunday afternoon. She was in great health. Forty-eight hours later, on a Tuesday afternoon, I was at school. A teacher came into the classroom where I was working and said, "Laura, I need you to come out into the hall for a moment." I did not think much about the request. However, as soon as I stepped into the hallway, I saw my mom. Now, my mom is a teacher, so she should have been at her school. Knowing that something was wrong, I said, "Mom?" It was the same as asking, "What is going on? Why are you here? What has happened?" Through tears she told me that her mom, my grandmother, the grandmother I talked with just forty-eight hours earlier, had died. Mom said, "She died in her sleep last night." I went into shock. I could not cry or respond with words. I turned around, went into the classroom, and grabbed my things.

The next day my dad, Rob, and I went to Aunt Mary's funeral while my mom stayed home to plan her own mother's funeral. As soon as Aunt Mary's funeral was over, my dad, Rob, and I drove the several hours back to my grandmother's house, which was full of friends and family. The very next day was the funeral for my grandmother. Obviously, it was a horrible time of shock, sadness, and grief that, unfortunately, was not over. One month later my other grandmother fell and broke her hip. As so often happens, the broken hip turned into many other health problems for my grandmother. So after breaking her hip she spent the next three months in the hospital before dying. So, in a six-month span, I lost my dog, great aunt, and both grandmothers. They each played a significant role in my life, and their deaths were life changing.

NEEDLESS TO SAY, THOSE SIX MONTHS WERE AN INTENSE TIME OF GRIEF. I GRIEVED THEIR DEATH AS WELL AS CONTINUING TO GRIEVE THE DETERIORATION OF MY SIGHT.

Needless to say, those six months were an intense time of grief. I grieved their death as well as continuing to grieve the deterioration of my sight. Most days during that six-month period I continued to feel that I was swimming against an ocean current, and doing so all alone. You know that feeling when you are convinced that you are going to drown in the circumstances of life? You are experiencing problems in so many different ways that it seems like life is more than you can handle and you will not survive. That is how I felt. Yet having received incredible actions of courage, determination, and perseverance in years past, I knew that, once again, my family would come together and support each other in such a difficult time. The actions of grit that we receive in the midst of one challenge will give us the strength and endurance to work through the difficulties of other adversities.

The results of all this displayed grit were experienced when family and friends helped me in various ways, and for that I am deeply grateful. I am also overwhelmed with gratitude for those moments when I was able to offer strength to others while also receiving strength. For example, the times that I helped a younger student find each of her classrooms at high school was an opportunity to offer strength to someone else. I was a junior and Erin a freshman. She was also visually impaired. Erin could use large print and magnifiers to complete her schoolwork. Just as I worked with a vision teacher to adapt my schoolwork to braille, Erin also worked with the same teacher to adapt her work to large print. One day Erin and I were in the same classroom working with our vision teacher. Since it was the middle of December, I asked her about the classes she was going to take when the new semester started in January. She named each class and then said, "I have no clue where each of those classrooms are located." I instantly sat straight up in my chair and with complete confidence said, "Oh, Erin, I know where each of those classes are, and I can show you where they are located." With all the confidence of a high school junior, I turned to our teacher and said, "Can I show Erin each of the classrooms?" So into the halls we went. Erin and I went to each of her new classrooms. Then we walked to the front of the building and walked through her day just as she would do when the new semester started. Erin and I repeated the same process of walking through the new schedule for several weeks.

After the two-week winter break, we started back to school for the new semester. The first few days went by without any major problems. Erin did great because she knew where each of her classes was located. She found each class and was never late. Typically, for me, the start of a new semester was the most difficult time. I was anxious and panicky about everything. Would I find my classes? Would my teachers work with me? Would I have the time and energy to get all the work done? The worries and feelings of panic were endless. So as the semester started that particular January, I realized I was not as nervous about finding my classes. While I was still anxious, overall I was much more confident. About two weeks into the semester I suddenly realized what was causing me to be much more calm. It was the time spent with Erin! While I also took the time I needed to learn my own new classrooms, I spent just as much time showing Erin where her classrooms were found. Rather than sitting in a classroom working on school assignments and panicking about the upcoming semester, I spent time helping Erin so she would not be anxious about the new semester.

There I was, a high school junior, and I had just learned a lesson that would change my life. Yes, I was a person with a disability. I was now labeled different than my friends and different than the person I used to be. I was now an "other" in society. I was going through an intense grieving process as I adjusted to the new normal that was blindness. I was a person who was consumed by anxiety, fear, and depression while still trying to move forward in life. So what did I learn? What was the life lesson? In the midst of needing so much help physically, emotionally, and spiritually, I still had gifts to offer to the world. I was still a person of worth and value. I was a person who had been given gifts and strengths just like each person created. So just as my parents, other family members, and friends were my source of strength, I also had the ability to offer the same actions of courage and support to other people. I was able to help Erin as I showed her where her classes

So what did I learn? What was the life lesson? In the midst of needing so much help physically, emotionally, and spiritually, I still had gifts to offer to the world.

were located, and Erin was helping me remain calm as I started a new semester. It wasn't just one person doing the helping or one person receiving the help. Rather, my interaction with Erin was an equal process; both of us were being supported. For this lesson I learned as a high school junior, I am forever grateful. While the lesson learned was a huge moment for me, it takes a lifetime to continue living out a life with the delicate balance of receiving and giving help. Unfortunately, it is not as simple as a one-time action. Rather, it's a day-to-day process of living into the reality that we are people of value and worth. Even in the most traumatizing situations of difficulty and struggle, we are each people that matter enough to be supported and to offer support.

I am filled with gratitude for so many of these lessons. I am deeply grateful for my parents, brother, friends, teachers, and the community that chose to enter into the difficult life circumstances with me. They didn't say things like, "Oh wow, that is horrible for you. We hope life works out for you." Quite the opposite. My parents, brother, close friends, and teachers taught me the skills I needed so I could live a full life. They empowered me so I could live out a life of purpose and meaning.

When we think back over our times of our adversity and trauma, we realize we were being held and supported in ways we could not imagine. While it did in fact feel, at the time, like we were alone, there were countless actions of grit displayed for us, actions that fill us with gratitude. Rather than swimming in the ocean alone, against that current, there were people who were willing to jump in the water and throw us a life jacket so we did not drown. Actually, their actions provided something far greater than merely tossing us a life jacket. They *themselves* were our very life jacket. Mary giving me a hug and telling me I was going to make it through the first day of high school was a life jacket. The freshman class voting me homecoming princess and my brother and his friends joining me that Friday night—these were life jackets. Martha crying with me as I wrestled with the fact that God was not healing me instantly: a life jacket. My parents finding ways to adapt each Saturday football game: another life jacket. Showing Erin her new classrooms was a life jacket.

What have been your life jacket moments? Spend some time reflecting on those moments in which other people entered into your pain and difficult situations to provide a word or action that gave you the strength for one more moment.

This deep awareness of thankfulness and appreciation gives each of us the strength to continue living life regardless of the ongoing adversity we will face.

Chapter 5

Moving Forward with Independence and Confidence

There are times in life when we are completely consumed with our present circumstances, and yet we must think about and plan for the future. These moments are like having a foot in two worlds. We are focused on the world we are currently in while also spending time and energy thinking about our future reality.

I found myself in that very place during the spring of my high school junior year. I was consumed with continuing to feel both peace and fear as I worked through the grieving process of vision loss. At the same time, my family and I were going through the period of four significant deaths in our family. While I was completely overwhelmed with life, it was the very time that I needed to be planning and thinking about life after high school. It was the season of taking the SAT, thinking about colleges, and planning for the future. Of course, college was a huge focus for me. However, there was another tremendous decision I was facing. Would I use a cane or guide dog as I transitioned to college life? In high school I refused to use a cane. Yes, I received the proper training and knew the correct techniques to use a cane. I knew how to safely cross a street with a cane. I also knew how and felt comfortable navigating different surroundings, such as sidewalks, stairs, and indoor places. Having the proper training and ability to use a cane and actually using a cane, however, are two totally different things! As a high schooler, I refused to use a cane because it made me stand out even more and labeled me as different. Now, in my high school of about twelve hundred students, everyone knew I was having vision problems. There was no secret about that! Even though I was aware that everyone knew, I still did not want to look different. I wanted to look like everyone else. While I knew I could get by without a cane in high school, I knew better than anyone else that I could not use the same approach in college and for the rest of my life. So there I was, a junior in high school, and I knew I had to seriously consider whether I would use a cane or guide dog in my future.

YOU KNOW HOW MAKING ONE BIG LIFE DECISION OPENS THE DOOR FOR THEN HAVING WHAT SEEMS A MILLION OTHER SMALLER DECISIONS TO MAKE? WELL, I WAS AT THAT POINT.

There are pros and cons to each decision. It is totally a matter of preference whether someone who is blind decides to use a cane or guide dog. It is not a matter of a right choice or a wrong choice; it is completely up to the individual. After much consideration and weighing of all my options, I decided on a guide dog. The next big round of questions and decisions included: When would I get the dog? What school would I attend to receive the dog? What did I need to learn to begin working with a guide dog? You know how making one big life decision opens the door for then having what seems a million other smaller decisions to make? Well, I was at that point. I had decided to get a guide dog. I now had many other questions that needed answers.

Thankfully, I was proficient at using a screen reader on a computer by this point. So I spent every minute that I could on the computer researching guide dogs and guide dog schools. I joined different guide dog user email groups so I could learn what it was like to have such a dog. I would spend hours talking to guide dog users on Instant Messenger. I was excited and yet nervous. I was again experiencing a range of emotions. I was energized and excited about the possibility of life with a guide dog, yet I was also terrified and nervous. After countless hours of talking to people and researching my options, I decided to apply to Guide Dogs for the Blind, which is in California. One Tuesday afternoon in the spring of my junior year, I walked outside, sat down on the front porch steps, and made the phone call to Guide Dogs for the Blind. I sat there on the top step holding the phone, feeling both excited and scared. My heart was racing and my breathing was getting more shallow. After dialing, the phone rang a few times. My heart was racing even faster now and my breathing was getting even more shallow. Finally someone on the other end of the call answered. "Guide Dogs for the Blind. May I help you?" I took a deep breath and said, "Yes, I need to request an application form, please." The woman said, "Sure. What is your name and address?" I thought to myself, *Good question, Lady!* I was

> I WAS ENERGIZED AND EXCITED ABOUT THE POSSIBILITY OF LIFE WITH A GUIDE DOG, YET I WAS ALSO TERRIFIED AND NERVOUS.

so afraid that I could barely tell her the information. She then said, "OK. Thank you. We will mail you the application form. Have a great day! Good-bye." And she hung up.

That call was all of about ninety seconds, yet it was one of the most important phone calls I had made. Why was I so excited and yet nervous? All I was doing was asking for an application form. What was the big deal? The phone call was monumental for several reasons. Making the decision to get a guide dog meant I was moving through the initial grieving process in such a way that allowed me to continue to live life rather than being hopeless and overcome by vision loss. Making that phone call meant I was moving forward with my life. The call meant I was willing to do what I needed to to have the mobility to navigate college safely in the future. This was a moment in which I had to make a decision for myself that would empower my life. These types of decision are those that no one else can make for us. Yes, family and friends are a huge part of the discernment process. They are a huge part of the reason we are able to make the empower-ing decision. And yet, they cannot make the choice for us. Ultimately, we have to make the decision. We have to believe that we are worthy enough and we matter enough to make choices that will equip our lives with the resources we need. Remember those life jacket moments in our lives? Those mo-ments when people and their very actions are the life jackets that give us the strength to move forward? Well, there are also times when we must choose to be our *own* life jacket. The life jacket moments that we have received from others have now given us the strength and self-worth to rise up and be our own life jacket. Sitting there on that top step of our front porch, I chose to take all of the life jacket moments in my life and use them as strength to reach deep within myself for the courage to call and ask for a guide dog application to be sent to my home.

Dr. Brene Brown, in her book *Daring Greatly* writes that choosing to have courage is not comfortable. Indeed, there is nothing easy or comfortable about having to display courage.[4] Yet choosing to make those life jacket decisions for our own self is empowering beyond words. Through those moments and actions of courage we are choosing to know and believe that we are each worthy individuals.

Similar to the grieving process, providing your own life jacket is not a linear process. There is not one huge defining moment in our lives where we decide that, from this point forward, we will always have the ability to be our own life jacket and no longer need the support and encouragement of others. Rather, it is a constant process of receiving support from others and receiving support within ourselves. As a high school student, I thought I would receive all of this help to get through the grieving process and then live life on my own strength. As a seventeen-year-old, I did not realize that anyone, sighted or blind, needs the healthy balance of receiving support from others as well as choosing to rely on their own inner strength.

Making that call to request an application was a life jacket moment for me. Mailing in the completed application was another important moment in my life. Once I had completed the written form, gathered the reference letters, and received a letter from my orientation and mobility instructor, the application was ready. Just like calling to request the application, I was nervous. It was a summer afternoon in July and Rob was leaving our house for a few errands. Right before he walked out the door I said, "Oh, will you mail my application?" He said, "Sure. Where is it?" I ran to the dining room table, grabbed the envelope, and handed it to Rob. The same feeling I had when I first made that phone call came flooding back. It was the feeling of a racing heart and shallow breathing. I nervously said, "Now, you know where the post office is, right? You know which box to put the envelope in?" In that most brotherly way, Rob said, "Yes, Laura." We had only been living in the same town and going to the same post office our entire lives!

Despite all my nervousness, I was choosing to respond to my life situation with courage. I was choosing to depend on the truth that I could make choices that would equip me to live a life of meaning and purpose. Those actions of courage and strength are not easy; they often feel uncomfortable or awkward. Just like that moment when my brother left for the post office with my application. Part of me was excited and could not wait to receive a guide dog. Another part of me was scared and frustrated, as I had many questions. Am I making the right decision? Will I like having a guide dog? Will a dog really help me? Why in the world am I applying for a dog? Why am I in the situation that forces me to think about using a cane or a guide dog? Choosing to have strength and courage is not easy, yet it is necessary for our very survival.

A few weeks later, I received a call that my written application had been accepted. I was ready for the second part of the application, which was a home interview. So, on my eighteenth birthday, I stayed home from school for my home interview. Now, I had prepared intensely for this interview. I knew I would have to walk a designated route with my cane to show the instructor I had the necessary skills to navigate independently. I had the perfect route planned. I even met with my orientation and mobility instructor so she could watch me and give me feedback. You know how it is when you want everything to be perfect? You exhaust yourself trying to make sure everything goes well. The day of the interview arrived, it was 9 in the morning, and an instructor from the guide dog school would be arriving at any minute. I was pacing the house, once again nervous and excited. I wanted things to go perfectly. I was worried that our 18-month-old black lab would not behave and I would fail the interview. Our black lab had nothing to do with the interview, and she could not cause me to fail. However, you know how it is in those moments. Your thoughts are racing, and you think of every reason imaginable that you are going to fail.

The doorbell rang and I opened the door to greet the instructor. We took seats in our living room, and about five minutes into the interview the doorbell rang. I continued to talk with the instructor while my dad answered the door. And what did he open the door to find? A huge bouquet of flowers my cousins had sent for my birthday. I could have melted into the couch at that moment. Again, my mind went to that place of, *Oh, this is over. I am really not going to pass now.* Was there an ounce of truth in that thought? Of course not! We continued with the interview and, about three minutes later, the doorbell rang and it was a man who was coming to look at a room in our house that he was going to paint. At this point I thought, *Seriously, this interview is over! There is no need to even melt into the couch at this point. I can just get up and leave now!* So again, for the third time we continued with the interview.

Then we came to the time when the instructor wanted to

see me walk with the cane. I explained to him that there was a neighborhood close by where we could go. He quickly said, "Oh no. Let's stay right here. Walk to the top of your street and then we will decide which direction to walk." I was thinking, *You have got to be kidding me! Really?* I planned out the perfect route. I even had someone give me feedback so I would not make any mistakes, and now you are telling me we are going to stay right here? I continued to convince myself that my perfect planned-out interview was going all wrong and there was no way I would ever get a guide dog!

Still, I did as the man said and we walked my neighborhood. The walk went well. Once we were back at my house he told me he would send in his report and I would hear back from the school. Needless to say, I was excited, but completely undone that the interview had not gone as I had perfectly planned in my mind. Were any of the interruptions going to affect the school's decision? Of course not! But in my eighteen-year-old mind, it was a much bigger deal. Thankfully, a month later, I received an email that I had been accepted to the guide dog class that would be held in February. I would go to California and spend a month at guide dog school. To say I was excited is a huge understatement. I had made the decision to get a guide dog, and that decision was now final. I would indeed be receiving a guide dog to help me physically navigate life safely. The one act of courage that I took back in the spring to call for an application had resulted in the great news that I was, for sure, going to get a guide dog. Each life jacket moment in our lives weaves with other moments to bring forth actions of courage, strength, and perseverance. It is not one single action; rather, it is the hundreds of small decisions we make on a daily basis to live a life of grit.

* * * * * * *

All the small acts of courage that I took when I researched and planned out getting a guide dog were being woven together. As a result, I found myself sitting in the San Francisco airport one February afternoon. Five others, who were going to be in my guide dog class, had arrived around the same time. Once we were assembled, one of the class instructors drove us to the campus. The moment of pulling into that campus is etched in my mind forever. As we entered the grounds, the dogs started barking. Literally, more than two hundred dogs were barking. My heart stopped. I thought to myself that one of the dogs barking was going to be *my* guide dog. *What have I done?* I am sitting in a van with six strangers at a guide dog school and I am three thousand miles from home. All those moments of feeling excited and confident were gone. I was now terrified. As we entered the dorm where we would each spend the next month, an instructor came up to me and said, "Hi, Laura. I am going to show you to your room." We walked the hall and entered a room on the right. The instructor then took the next ten minutes describing to me where everything was in the room. Well, she could have said that there was an elephant and a giraffe in the room and I would have said, "Oh, OK! Thank you." I have no clue what she said during those ten minutes. I did not have the mental capacity to receive any of the information. I was still terrified and anxious. The instructor said, "Do you have any questions?" I shook my head no. She said, "OK. You have a few minutes to get your things unpacked and then I will be back."

As soon as she walked from the room and closed the door, I collapsed on the bed and called my brother. Thankfully, Rob answered. I could not get a word out. I just started sobbing. For the next few minutes, I sat on the bed crying while I listened to him tell me I was going to be fine. I had made the right decision. I was not going to give up. I was going to have a great experience. Even though in the moment I did not believe a word he was saying, I knew, deep down, Rob was right.

My brother's words were a life jacket in that situation. I needed his supportive words to give me the strength and courage as I felt scared and nervous. Our lives constantly fluctuate between possessing the needed determination and perseverance within ourselves and needing the courage and tenacity of other people. And in reality, we often experience the grit within ourselves and the grit of others at the same time. But rather than there being a clearly defined difference between the two, we are often tapping into the strength within ourselves while also receiving the strength of others. We can all name various times and situations when we were scared and afraid and needed great courage. In those moments of fear, we need people around us to support us with actions of strength and encouragement. Just as I sat there in the dorm sobbing while listening to my brother, I was, at the same time, showing actions of perseverance. I was choosing to persevere and move forward in the face of the difficult reality of my new normal. In the moment I felt anything but strong. I needed someone in my support system to remind me that I was indeed persevering.

IN THE MOMENT I FELT ANYTHING BUT STRONG. I NEEDED SOMEONE IN MY SUPPORT SYSTEM TO REMIND ME THAT I WAS INDEED PERSEVERING.

The next three days went by quickly. The twenty-four other students and I in this class spent our days learning how to work with a guide dog. We also spent time walking different routes with instructors as we prepared to receive our dogs. Finally, the day that we would receive our dog arrived. It was a Wednesday and I was back to being excited and nervous. We spent the morning walking routes. We would get our dogs after lunch. All twenty-five of us, plus our instructors, were sitting in one big room. The instructor was going to read our names and tell us what breed of dog we would receive and the name of the dog. Then we would all go back to our rooms and one of the instructors would come and get us to receive our dog. I sat there nervous but excited. I was ready. I could not wait one more minute to find out about my dog. Unlike the moment when I first heard the dogs barking, I was now excited. My heart was racing and I could not sit still. The instructor started reading the names. When she called mine, I froze. As she continued—"Laura, you are getting a . . . "—my mind just stopped. Then, she was on to the next person. All I could remember was that my dog would be a Labrador, which was not very helpful since I already knew the dog was going to be a lab or golden retriever! Once the instructor was through with all the names, everyone headed to their rooms. Everyone, that is, but me. I headed toward the instructor to find out about my dog. About three steps forward, I ran right into a coffee table that was in front of a couch. Let me assure you that running into the table had nothing to do with my vision! It had everything to do with my nerves! My instructor said, "Laura?" and we both started laughing. She knew as well as I did that I saw the table, that I was simply so nervous I was shaking.

I told her I could not remember anything she said. "What kind of dog am I getting?" I asked. She took a quick look at her sheet and said, "You are getting a female black lab named Jira. I will come to get you shortly." So I headed to my room to wait. After a few minutes, there was a knock on my door; it was my instructor. We walked together down the hall to her office. She said, "I will be back in one minute with Jira." It felt like years that I sat there waiting. Finally, she reentered the room with a small black lab. She said, "Laura, meet Jira." I said, "Hey, Jira."

She walked right by me, grabbed a bone, and started chewing! After a few minutes the instructor said, "Let's go back to your room. You and Jira can play for about an hour." We started walking down the hall and, like any other twenty-two-month-old lab, Jira started pulling on the leash. I turned around and looked at my instructor with a look that said: What do I do? She is pulling. Now, I had only been around dogs my entire life. So I knew how to walk a dog on a leash! I knew how to correct the dog so she would heel. But walking down the hall with my new guide dog, I was still quite nervous. Rather than holding the leash like a confident dog handler, I was holding that leash as if Jira was breakable, fragile. Once in my room, the instructor had said, I should spend the time playing with Jira. I sat on the floor beside her. What did she do? She ran right to the bones in my room and started chewing! I thought, *Oh, this bonding process is not going well! We are supposed to spend the next hour bonding, and she doesn't even care that I exist!* Then a few minutes later, without any warning, Jira walked over to where I was sitting on the floor, licked my eyes, and went right back to chewing her bones. And I sat there and began crying. Not tears of terror or anxiety as I experienced that first day. Rather, these were tears of thanksgiving and joy. I was overwhelmed with gratitude.

"Yes, girl, you are going to be my eyes. You are my eyes and you are going to help me move forward in life," I said to Jira. *Together*, I thought, *we will adapt to this new normal.*

The next morning it was time to take our dogs on their first walk. It would be the first time we would walk with them guiding us. I was sitting with Jira on the bus that had transported us to the route and was waiting my turn. It was about 50 degrees and raining. The instructor called my name. Jira and I stood and joined my instructor on the sidewalk; once again, I was quite nervous. The instructor gave me a short route and said, "I will be right here behind you." So, with rain pouring down, I picked up the harness and said, "Jira, forward." She started walking forward and, of course, I did too. We walked about two blocks. Having Jira guide me felt completely awkward, and yet not horrible. We completed our walk and got back on the bus, where I waited for the other students. I sat there, just numb. I was not afraid, but I was not confident either. I was not completely sold on the idea that this dog was going to guide me and keep me safe. Yet I was optimistic and excited about the possibility. Sitting there with Jira after our first walk was one of those moments in life when we just have to keep moving forward, even though it does not feel comfortable. Often, as we adapt and work through adversity to the new normal, the new way of living feels strange. The new way of living or thinking feels uncomfortable, awkward. We find ourselves stuck between knowing that we cannot live as we used to live while being especially aware that our present is not natural to our typical way of living. Adjusting to the new normal is somewhat like putting on a new pair of tennis shoes. The shoes feel stiff, uncomfortable. It is not until we wear the shoes for awhile that they start to feel molded and natural around our feet.

After that first walk with Jira, I slowly became more confident as I lived into the gift of Jira becoming my eyes. One particular day brought a defining moment in our four weeks of training. Each week the routes that we walked with our dogs got longer and more difficult. On the third week of training we went to the San Francisco Business District. It was 8:30 in the morning on a cloudy, misty Wednesday in late February, and I was standing on the sidewalk with one of the instructors. She gave me a route I would walk and told me I was on my own. She was going to be behind me, but I would walk the route as if she was not there. Since it was the third week, I was confident and ready to go. We had already done a few routes in San Francisco, routes that included public transportation. I stood there on the sidewalk, by now completely confident, and said, "OK. No problem."

So I picked up the harness and said, "Jira, forward." We walked the first block with no difficulty. As we came to the end of the block, Jira slowed as we approached the curb. I stood at the intersection and listened for the flow of traffic. Once I knew it was safe to cross the street, I said, "Jira, forward." We both stepped off the curb. After I took two steps off the curb, Jira suddenly jumped back on the curb, forcing me back up on the sidewalk. As soon as my feet hit the sidewalk, a car went by the very point where Jira and I had been standing. Obviously, I stood there on the curb terrified and shaking. What just happened? As my trainer approached me, I turned and asked, "What did I do wrong?" She quickly said, "Laura, you did not do anything wrong. Jira did everything right." She told me the car had turned right on red illegally. Jira had seen the car coming and quickly got me from harm's way. As an eighteen-year-old standing on the corner of a busy intersection in the San Francisco Business District, at 8:45 in the morning, three thousand miles from home, there are not adequate words to describe that moment. Again, the two words that leap to my mind are grit and gratitude. Grit: the support

OBVIOUSLY, I STOOD THERE ON THE CURB TERRIFIED AND SHAKING. WHAT JUST HAPPENED? AS MY TRAINER APPROACHED ME, I TURNED AND ASKED, "WHAT DID I DO WRONG?" SHE QUICKLY SAID, "LAURA, YOU DID NOT DO ANYTHING WRONG. JIRA DID EVERYTHING RIGHT."

system around me of family, friends, and community provided a strong foundation of determination, perseverance, and courage. The foundation of strength and tenacity empowered me in those first few years of grieving as well as building a foundation that would last my entire life. I was growing into the ability to apply those characteristics of determination and courage for myself. So, standing there on the curb in San Francisco, terrified and shaking, Jira showed me through her actions that she, too, had incredible strength and courage. She indeed had what it took to be my eyes. She knew just how to keep me safe and be my guide. I could indeed trust her with my safety. Even though I was terrified because of the reality of the specific situation, I was equally full of confidence as I knew, in that moment, that Jira would empower me to safely navigate college and the years to come.

JIRA SHOWED ME THROUGH HER ACTIONS THAT SHE, TOO, HAD INCREDIBLE STRENGTH AND COURAGE. SHE INDEED HAD WHAT IT TOOK TO BE MY EYES.

Together, Jira and I had the grit to move forward in life.

Gratitude applied to that moment every bit as much as grit. I was overwhelmed with gratefulness for the dog who had just saved me from being hit by a car. I was thankful for the dog that now—and in the future—would guide me each and every day. As we strive to overcome and work through the adversity and trauma in our lives, there are the defining moments that show us we can indeed continue through life. It is like the life jacket moments turn into moments of sitting in a small boat feeling the waves roll beneath us. When the obstacles and setbacks first occur, life feels like we are out in the middle of the ocean swimming against that strong current. We are only able to keep swimming and stay afloat by the life jacket that has been given us through the supportive actions of others. After what seems like forever, we are finally able to transition from swimming against the current with our life jacket to sitting in a boat feeling the waves roll under the boat. We are no longer drowning in the waves of adversity and trauma. Rather, we are equipped with strength, courage, and perseverance. Yes, the difficulties continue to affect our lives. The waves of adversity have not changed. What has changed is our ability to apply grit and gratitude.

I was still facing a stark reality—my sight was getting worse and worse. I was now living a new normal. But I was not just surviving so I would not drown in an ocean of adversity. I was now entering a new time when I could move forward.

* * * * * * *

The four weeks in this school were a time of fear and nervousness as I entered the new world of having a guide dog. The four weeks also were a time of confidence and strength. Many people who had guide dogs told me that receiving a guide dog would be like getting my sight back. Of course, I thought that statement was the most ridiculous thing I had heard! I would think to myself, *I will tell you just what it would be like to get my sight back.* But it turns out they were right. A guide dog did not give me my physical sight. But a guide dog does give me the ability to live with incredible confidence and freedom.

While guide dog school was intense and life changing, the time was also full of laughter and joy. For example, during that first week when we received our dogs, I was standing in the hall by my room working with an instructor on basic commands. I was focused and concentrating hard on learning all the commands I would give Jira. I stood there going through some of the commands, such as "Jira forward," "Jira heel," "Jira left," and "Jira right." Suddenly the instructor stopped me. He walked over to me and said, "Laura, I have one major concern." My heart stopped. I froze. I thought to myself, *Oh no, I have failed! Guide dog school is over! They are going to put me on a plane back home!* Then, in a serious voice, the instructor said, "Laura, each of these words are one syllable. Jira cannot follow your commands with your southern accent that is making each word twelve syllables!"

We both burst out laughing! He added, "You are doing great with the commands. Go take a break and get ready for our next session." Still laughing, I told him I would work on those syllables! I would not make any promises, but I would try to get the twelve syllables down to six!

THEN, IN A SERIOUS VOICE, THE INSTRUCTOR SAID, "LAURA, EACH OF THESE WORDS ARE ONE SYLLABLE. JIRA CANNOT FOLLOW YOUR COMMANDS WITH YOUR SOUTHERN ACCENT THAT IS MAKING EACH WORD TWELVE SYLLABLES!"

There continued to be many moments of laughter that balanced the intensity of the training. There were also times of joy. For example, the night in training that I talked to Jira's puppy raisers was a joyous time. It was toward the end of training and we were given the contact info for the people who had raised our dogs. It was a joy, a gift, to share with Jira's puppy raisers how she was doing in class. We talked for awhile, and then they told me they would be at the graduation. Indeed, meeting Caroline and Jeff was wonderful! On graduation day, they were there to see the dog they had raised for sixteen months. The last time they had seen Jira she was eighteen months old and did not know a single guide dog command. Now she was twenty-two months and a true guide dog! They were also meeting me, the person who was partnered with Jira. It was a day of joy and gratitude. That day was the beginning of a friendship that would grow and continue forever; we were now connected beyond words by a wonderful dog that had changed both of our lives.

THAT DAY WAS THE BEGINNING OF A FRIENDSHIP THAT WOULD GROW AND CONTINUE FOREVER; WE WERE NOW CONNECTED BEYOND WORDS BY A WONDERFUL DOG THAT HAD CHANGED BOTH OF OUR LIVES.

Chapter 6

Fully Embracing
the Present Reality

As we experience difficulties, obstacles, and adversity, there comes a time when we move from barely surviving to now living in the new normal. Life is different. Life is not the same as it used to be. It is not a matter of returning to the way life was before the difficulties. Rather, it is a matter of moving forward, living into the present reality. Transitioning to our new normal is like now living life securely in a boat on a rolling ocean. Rather than living life swimming against the strong ocean current, we are confidently sitting in the boat as it powers through the deep, wide ocean waters. College was that time for me, a period when I transitioned from swimming in the ocean with a life jacket to being securely in the boat. It was a time when I learned to be comfortable and confident in my own skin while also becoming even more aware of the stigma of having a disability.

Like so many high school students, I spent the spring of

my junior year and fall of my senior year deciding where I would attend college. My parents and I spent countless hours researching schools well equipped for people with disabilities. After much research and visiting several universities, I decided to attend Arizona State University. Since adapting to life without sight was still so new, I knew I needed to attend a school that could both teach me and empower me as a student with a disability. Once I was accepted to Arizona State, I decided to graduate from high school a semester early so I could attend guide dog school for a month, adjust to life with a guide dog, and prepare for college before starting that fall.

During my years in college, I became comfortable in my own skin as a person who is blind. Throughout middle school and high school I worked hard to hide my blindness. I exhausted myself trying to cover up my reality. Preparing for and going through the college years was a time of learning how to accept myself.

I first learned how to be comfortable in my own skin by being part of an environment where having a disability was normalized. For example, learning about resources that were available to students with disabilities so they could be integrated into the typical college classroom environment was incredibly empowering. Before starting classes, I had a meeting with my disability coordinator, Terri. I sat in her office as Terri told me about all the accommodations that were available. She said, "Laura, each of your textbooks will be in electronic format that you can read on your computer or in braille. You will arrange with each of your professors to have a student in each class who will take notes for you, and any class handouts will be emailed to you by the professor. You will take all of your exams here at the testing center in the Disability Resource Center. Each test will be in electronic format on the computer or in braille and you will have double the time for each exam." I sat there thinking, *Wow! So maybe I am not the first blind person to ever walk on earth!* Terri was rattling off this information like it was common knowledge. No, I was not the first blind person to walk the face of the earth. In fact, I was not even the first person who was blind to attend college! Terri's entire job was to be the disability coordinator for students who were low vision or blind. In this role, she was able to teach me and empower me with the resources I needed. As I sat there in Terri's office, learning about all the different ways classes could be adapted for people who are blind, I gained so much confidence. Suddenly, I was not the only one! I was not the only Arizona State University student who was blind. Words cannot begin to express how healing and normalizing it was to be received as any other student.

Often when we experience adversity, obstacles, or trauma, we feel isolated. It feels as though we are the only ones in the world who have experienced what we are going through. It can all feel incredibly isolating. It doesn't feel that way because we are physically isolated from others, but because we are isolated in our life situation. So I sat there in Terri's office gaining so much confidence as I anticipated the start of college. I was not isolated. Rather, the fact was that my disability was completely normalized.[5]

Meeting with Terri was incredibly healing as I learned about the many resources available to me as a student who is blind. The isolation that I felt also decreased as Terri introduced me to many other students who were low vision or blind. Meeting the other students was a great source of encouragement. As I met them and witnessed the ways they were living an extremely normal life, I gained confidence and strength.

One of the students Terri introduced me to was Virginia, a graduate student in her mid-thirties. Virginia also lost a significant amount of sight as a teenager. So she too knew what it was like to adapt to life with limited sight. Virginia was a powerful mentor figure in my life. She taught me how to manage the demands of college classes, live life with a guide dog, and be comfortable and confident in my own skin. Virginia taught me how to live a life of grit as I grew in my confidence. One day as I was finishing a meeting with Terri, Virginia walked in Terri's office. She said, "Laura, I am finished with class for the day. Are you going back to your apartment?" I told her I was, and she said, "Great! Let's go back together." I was thinking, *Oh, this is wonderful!* Virginia and I lived close to each other. So we would often walk together or take the bus together. As a new guide dog user, I was not completely confident working with Jira. Being with Virginia was a gift because I could learn from the ways she and her dog worked together. So when she said we could go back together, I was relieved and excited. Then she said, "Laura, I want you to lead on the way back. I will follow you. Since we have done this route several times, I want you to try it on your own."

I was once again both nervous and excited at the same time. Could I do it? Did I have confidence in myself and in Jira and me as a team? Then all the "what-ifs" started racing through my mind. At the same time, thoughts of proving to myself that I did indeed have the confidence, that Jira and I were a strong team, also were racing through my head. So, both excited and anxious, I said, "OK, I will give it a try!"

A few minutes later Virginia and I were walking through

campus to our bus stop. Once we were standing at the stop waiting for the bus to pull up, I took a big, deep breath and said, "So we made it this far!" I gained courage just in those few blocks of campus we had walked and the one street we had crossed. When the bus pulled up, I said confidently, "OK, Virginia, here is our bus. Let's go." I was doing this whole leading thing, and doing it perfectly—or so I thought. Then, as good mentors do, Virginia quietly asked, "Laura, so this is the bus that we want? This is the bus that will get us back?" Well, with those questions and the tone of her voice, I knew I needed to rethink my decision. I then realized that, obviously, multiple buses came by this stop, so I could not just jump on the first one that arrived. After listening closely to the bus number, I knew that we needed to continue to wait. After getting on the correct bus and getting off at our stop, I turned to Virginia and said, "Well? So how did I do?" Virginia said, "Good job, Laura. You have what you need. Each day you are gaining confidence as you work with Jira. Keep it up and you will be just fine. Now let's go get lunch." My first response was, "Do I have to lead again?" She laughed and said, "Yes! You lead to lunch and then I will lead once we are going home." I said, "Deal!"

Virginia constantly pushed me to rely on the grit that I had within myself. She knew firsthand what it was like to adapt to life without sight as well as adapting to life with a guide dog. She knew the value of developing the characteristics of courage, determination, and perseverance as I navigated this new chapter in life. Some days Virginia was teaching me how to become more confident, like that afternoon leaving campus. Other days, she was teaching me through her actions how to live a normal life. Virginia and I would often get ice cream or a manicure or pedicure together. Regardless of what we were doing, I was becoming more and more comfortable as a person who is blind. The feelings of isolation were quickly fading.

When we go through difficult challenges and obstacles, we feel like we are alone. It feels like we are the only ones. It seems as though no one could possibly understand what we are going through. Then we interact with someone who can identify with our challenges and struggles. We slowly realize that, in fact, we are not the only ones. We can share the frustration, anger, sadness, and fear with someone in a similar situation. We can also share the grit of courage, determination, and tenacity that it requires to overcome the difficulties and adversities. As we share both the fears and determination, we gain incredible confidence to accept ourselves and be comfortable with who we are. I learned how to accept myself and be comfortable in my own skin as I was around other people who were blind and living a normal life. I also gained confidence and acceptance as I was integrated with other college students.

As we experience adversity, it is invaluable to surround ourselves with people who can identify with and relate to our situation. As we interact with people who understand how we feel, we do not feel isolated and alone in our struggles. We also receive healing from interacting with many other types of people, during times when the focus is not on our struggles or adversity.

AS WE INTERACT WITH PEOPLE WHO UNDERSTAND HOW WE FEEL, WE DO NOT FEEL ISOLATED AND ALONE IN OUR STRUGGLES. WE ALSO RECEIVE HEALING FROM INTERACTING WITH MANY OTHER TYPES OF PEOPLE, THOSE TIMES WHEN THE FOCUS IS NOT ON OUR STRUGGLES OR ADVERSITY.

I took a summer English class before the fall of my freshman year began. The first day of class a girl named Julie sat next to me. We started talking before and after class, all of the basic questions: "Where are you from?" "What year are you?" Each day we continued to talk. At the end of the second week, Julie walked over to me as she was leaving class and said, "Hey Laura, do you want to get together this weekend? Friends and I are getting together and I would love for you to come." I said, "Yes, that would be great." So we exchanged numbers and said we would be in touch. Why was that interaction a healing one? I was just sitting there, like usual, packing up my laptop and notebook and getting ready to leave the classroom. The interaction with Julie that Friday afternoon was empowering because it taught me that I am a whole person. I am not just blind. Until that point in my life, everyone around me knew me as a person who was sighted and had transitioned to being blind. They knew me as both sighted and blind. I had spent my life in a place where everyone knew me since I was born.

THE INTERACTION WITH JULIE THAT FRIDAY AFTERNOON WAS EMPOWERING BECAUSE IT TAUGHT ME THAT I AM A WHOLE PERSON. I AM NOT JUST BLIND.

My parents grew up with most of my friends' parents. They all knew each other.

But now, here, I was in this new college environment with people who would only know me as a person who is blind. So I was hesitant and uncomfortable. What would they think of me? How would I be treated? I was trying to be comfortable with myself as a person with a disability while also navigating a new environment. So when Julie invited me to get together, I realized she was not inviting me because I was blind. She was not inviting me because she felt sorry for me. There were plenty of other people in the classroom we had both talked with. I was not the only person she could have asked. So what was the reason? Julie and I had much in common. We had fun talking, laughing, and—let's be honest—complaining about summer English class! No, Julie did not feel sorry for me because of my blindness. She wanted to get together because we had connected as friends. For the rest of the summer we had fun getting together after class, going to the pool, going shopping, going to parties, and taking road trips. Julie was a great friend that summer as well as throughout college. Yes, she was aware I was blind. And she helped me whenever I needed it. But no, my blindness did not often come up in conversations. And yes, our friendship was based on who we were as whole people.

Julie taught me the value of accepting myself just as I am. I am a person who is blind. I have a disability. But I am so much more than just blind or disabled. I am a whole person. I have strengths and weaknesses as well as gifts and areas of struggle. We are each people who are more than our difficulties and challenges. As the adversity that we face consumes us and requires so much of our energy, we are also humans with different personalities and gifts. While it is easy to zoom in on the challenge, it is healing to zoom out and become aware of the entire picture of our lives. What a gift it is when we interact with people like Julie. People who teach us to view ourselves as whole individuals. People who show us that we have gifts and talents to offer. There are not words to express my deep gratitude for people like Julie. Our gratitude can only be expressed by receiving their acceptance of our lives, believing that we are indeed whole individuals, and viewing others as whole people.

There are people in our lives who teach us and show us the value of accepting ourselves as a whole person. There are also events that help us realize our lives do not just revolve around our obstacles and challenges. Life continues to move forward, and it reminds us that we too can continue in the new normal. Move-in day of freshman year was one of those powerful moments in my life. It was a Thursday in mid-August and the temperature was well above 100 degrees; my parents and I were moving me into my dorm room. You know how it goes: the day starts with everyone and their parents excited and happy. Then, as the carloads continue and the afternoon sun continues to beat down, everyone is, well, not quite as energized. The conversation quickly turns to something like: Is there much more to unpack? Are we done yet? And finally, after many trips to the car and much work, everything is ready. The sheets and comforter are on the bed, the clothes are hung in the closet, the desk is put together, and the tiny microwave and refrigerator are plugged in and working! Later that night Julie and friends came over to see my room. As we talked, I was overwhelmed with a feeling of *normal.* I was more comfortable than ever in my new life situation. Yes, I was still blind. Yes, I was different than the other students in my dorm. And yes, I was starting college just like everyone else.

Accepting ourselves as we are and becoming comfortable in our new reality is hard. Living life in our new normal can be frustrating, discouraging, stressful, and exhausting. It is not a quick process. Rather, it is a slow progression of going back and forth as we get comfortable in our reality. It takes countless events of courage, determination, and perseverance to settle into our present situation. Becoming comfortable with who we are requires all the grit we can display, as well as tapping into as much as we can from our family, friends, mentors, strangers, and various life situations. The process is hard and exhausting, yet also healing and empowering.

During the college years I was able to become comfortable in my own skin as a person who is blind. As I learned from others who were blind, and living in an environment that was incredibly accepting of all people, my confidence greatly increased. While I received unbelievable strength and encouragement to live into the person that I was, there also was a point in college when I realized that being comfortable with myself was not only based on the people around me and the actions of others. Rather, being comfortable in my own reality meant that I also accepted myself regardless of the perceptions of other people. I quickly learned—and experienced—how people with disabilities often are treated differently. If being comfortable with who I am was going to be based on others' opinions of me, I was going to fluctuate between being extremely uncomfortable and at other times feeling incredibly accepted. One moment I was going to be shocked that I woke up and got out of bed, and the next moment I would be feeling like the most amazing person in the world. So I quickly learned that my self-confidence and self-acceptance could not come only from outside influences. It also needed to come from within myself. I had to choose to have plenty of grit within myself. And that grit had to be based on who I believed I was. That wasn't an easy decision. And it wasn't a decision I would only have to make once. Rather, it was a process that started in college and would be one that would have to continue forever. And it comes through both positive and negative experiences.

THAT GRIT HAD TO BE BASED ON WHO I BELIEVED I WAS. THAT WASN'T AN EASY DECISION. AND IT WASN'T A DECISION I WOULD ONLY HAVE TO MAKE ONCE.

As I had countless positive experiences at ASU, I also had negative ones; I quickly realized how people with disabilities are often viewed. One situation took place in the fall semester of my freshman year. One of my classes was Biology 101, which was held in a huge auditorium with several hundred students. It was the first day of class; I sat in the back row.

As I got out my laptop, another student came and sat beside me. She took one look at me and said, "Oh, great! You can be my project for the semester!" I thought to myself, *Seriously? Oh, I thought I was human. I am just an object?* Completely shocked, I looked at her with an expression of: What in the world do you mean by that? But I chose to say, "Hi. I am Laura." Desperately hoping that she would realize I was a human!

SHE TOOK ONE LOOK AT ME AND SAID, "OH, GREAT! YOU CAN BE MY PROJECT FOR THE SEMESTER!" I THOUGHT TO MYSELF, *SERIOUSLY? OH, I THOUGHT I WAS HUMAN. I AM JUST AN OBJECT?*

Another student in the class was going to be my note taker, so I was left feeling totally confused. The first girl responded by saying, "Hi. I am Caitlin. You can be my project this semester." I thought, *Does she just want to help me? Is she going to try to fix me so I will not be blind?* I simply answered, "I have everything that I need for this class, but if at some point I need help, I will let you know." In truth, I had no clue how to respond! I wanted to say anything but kind words. I was new at this whole responding-to-weird-comments thing. Throughout the semester she would speak to me, but she did not again bring up the statement that I would be her project! So I thought that maybe my response had worked.

Then, about three or four weeks before the semester ended, a friend came to class with Caitlin. She introduced me to her friend. The friend loudly said, "Wow! You look nothing like what I thought you were going to look like. Caitlin has been telling me about her project, and wow! You just look nothing like what I pictured in my mind all semester." I wanted to scream, *Yeah, because I am human. Not an object that is a project!* But rather than verbalize those thoughts, I just responded, "Oh really?"

In that strange encounter it would have been easy to not accept myself as a person who is blind. It would have been easy to get into the mind-set of: *Well, Caitlin does not view me as a full human, so why should I? She does not treat me with respect, so I guess I do not deserve respect.* Thankfully, I was in a place where I could acknowledge my anger and frustration and then choose to show grit instead. Through that whole situation, I had to choose to have courage and tenacity. Yes, I was hurt and frustrated by the comments. But yes, I could also continue to live into the fact that I accepted myself as a person who is blind regardless of the comments I received.

While in college I became close friends with Rebecca. She was a junior when I was a freshman. We were both from the Southeast and had a lot in common. Rebecca was also a guide dog user. Whenever we both had breaks between classes we would get together for coffee or lunch. One semester we had a Spanish class together. It was early in the semester. We met for coffee before class started, then we walked to class. Once in the classroom we sat next to each other. I pulled out my braille textbook while Rebecca got out her large print textbook. A few minutes before class began another student walked up and said, "Oh, I saw you two walking to class together. How cute that you blind girls can have a friend." Then, without waiting for our response, she walked away. I wanted to burst out crying and scream at that student all at the same time. Since the professor started the class, Rebecca and I did not have a chance to vent about the comment. I just shot her a quick look that said, What in the world just happened?

Rebecca was an incredible help to me as I adjusted to life with a guide dog. Since she already had her dog for several years, she knew the ins and outs. So I relied on her to help me become a confident handler. Rebecca also was such a great friend because she could relate to the frustrations and struggles of living life as a person with a disability. I could share aggravations that I experienced, such as the student in biology telling me I was her "project." Rebecca could understand since she, too, experienced the same reactions. Just as we deeply related to each other regarding blindness, we were such close friends because of other interests we had in common. Yes, we got to know each other because we were both students with disabilities. However, we had so much more that connected us. Often our conversations did not even revolve around being blind. Being new at living life with a disability, it never crossed my mind that someone would perceive that we were each other's only friend, or that we were friends just because of our blindness.

I had all of that class to stew in my anger and frustration. So when it ended I was ready to unload all my anger on Rebecca. Once we were outside we both started at the same time. "Could you believe that? Did you hear what I heard?" "Did she really say that? How ridiculous!" And we came up with a plan. We would not walk to class together and we would not sit together. We would show the student and the world that, no, we were not each other's only friend, and no, we were not friends just because of our blindness. So, for a few classes we did not go to class together and we did not sit together. But then, after a while, we both realized how pointless it was for us to continue trying to make this point. The student was going to think whatever she wanted! We were not going to change the perceptions of others simply by sitting away from each other in class. This frustrating experience in Spanish class taught me a valuable lesson. I learned to have courage and strength in who I was rather than allowing the perceptions of others to strip away my confidence. I had to feel my anger and then choose to know the truth that I did indeed have other friends. I was a friend with Rebecca because of much more than simply our blindness.

As we adjust to life in a new normal, we are incredibly susceptible to being influenced by the words and actions of others. Such comments and actions can cause us to have a range of reactions, everything from defensiveness, anger, and sadness to extreme frustration. How important it is for each of us to allow in those feelings and then choose to respond with grit. Instead of responding with an I-will-show-you attitude like Rebecca and I did for a few classes, it is healthy for us to respond with courage and strength. So, in that Spanish class, we finally decided to respond in just that way. We would again walk to class whenever we were together. We would also sit near each other when we could. Accepting any and all of the perceptions of others is difficult when adjusting to a new normal. Courage, strength, and tenacity are required so those perceptions do not crush our self-worth.

I also quickly learned that as a person with a disability, often people speak to you in a different tone. Now that I was blind and using a guide dog, many people talked to me differently; they didn't use normal tones and volumes. People would speak to me in a much louder voice. They also would speak to me in a much slower speed. The

IN COLLEGE, AND EVEN TO THIS DAY, I SOMETIMES WANT TO SCREAM, "I CAN HEAR YOU JUST FINE. I CAN UNDERSTAND YOUR WORDS JUST FINE. NO, SPEAKING SLOWER AND LOUDER IS NOT GOING TO HELP ME SEE YOU!"

tone becomes one of pity. In college, and even to this day, I sometimes want to scream, "I can hear you just fine. I can understand your words just fine. No, speaking slower and louder is not going to help me see you!" When I first noticed the pattern, I was sad, angry, and frustrated. I was sad because I was extremely aware of how people who are labeled as disabled are treated as less than other people. I was angry that I was being treated differently. Just a few years earlier, I did not have any of these challenges! I was frustrated because I was trying to work through the process of being comfortable with myself even while being treated as though I was "less than." So what was I going to do? There was no way I was going to control the actions of the world around me so that everyone would speak to me normally. But there was—and continues to be— one perspective that I can control. I can control my thoughts and actions. No, I cannot change how people react to me. Yes, I can change how I respond. For some time, the comments ate away at me. I would continue to feel sad, angry, frustrated. Then, through the help of others with disabilities as well as friends and family, my feelings changed. Rather than allowing each loud, slow conversation to take from my self-worth, I began to let myself experience the feelings of sadness, anger, and frustration. Then I would remind myself that I am fully human and can completely accept myself. Just because someone is speaking to me in a way that makes me feel "less than," I do not have to live in a way that is "less than."

I also learned to extend grace as people speak to me in a different way. Rather than thinking these are horrible, mean people, I know that in most situations they do not even realize they are speaking differently. Have I spoken to people in a way that said to them, "You are different"? Absolutely! Did I do it on purpose or to be harmful? Absolutely not! So I understand that the people speaking slower and louder to me are not trying to hurt me. Yet it takes constant work to keep these interactions from feeling like truth in our lives.

Dr. Brene Brown, in her book *Rising Strong,* writes about the value of having a one-inch-by-one-inch notecard. On the notecard you list the people who are closest to you. The people whose opinions you value.[6] So when we are struggling to live into our new normal, to accept ourselves fully in our new reality, how do we respond when people treat us differently? How do we respond when we are easily influenced by the words and actions of others? It is easy for our lives to become something like a scab that has just formed. The scab can easily be ripped open so that the raw, hurt area is exposed.

We respond by turning to those people listed on our notecard as well as turning toward ourselves. We choose to focus on the words and actions of those we trust most. The people who are closest to us and accept us just as we are. They provide us with courage and tenacity and love us as whole people as we go through the awkward transition of accepting our new normal. As we receive their actions of acceptance, we are also able to view ourselves as whole people. Yes, we are different because of the adversity we've faced and live with on a daily basis. Yes, we can know that we are worthy human beings even when we are being labeled differently.

YES, WE ARE DIFFERENT BECAUSE OF THE ADVERSITY WE'VE FACED AND LIVE WITH ON A DAILY BASIS. YES, WE CAN KNOW THAT WE ARE WORTHY HUMAN BEINGS EVEN WHEN WE ARE BEING LABELED DIFFERENTLY.

The strange comments I received from the person in Biology 101 referring to me as a project, and the other times people have spoken to me differently—these are hurtful. The interactions caused me to struggle as I adjusted to my new normal. But there was another reaction I received that negatively affected me—and this one hurt the most. The sadness, anger, and frustration went to a whole new level, a deeper level that penetrates the core of my being. I call it the invisible factor. These are situations when people completely ignore my existence. It is literally as though I am not physically present. Rather than talking to me as a person who happens to have a disability, the other person only talks to the person I am with. The first time I experienced the invisible factor I was at a restaurant with friends. After class, Julie and I went with other friends for lunch. We were sitting at a booth, each person discussing what we were going to order. The waitress came up to take our drink orders. She went around to each person. Then, when she got to me, she looked in the opposite direction that I was sitting and said to a friend across the table, "What would she like to drink?" *She?* I was instantly both shocked and defensive. You would have thought I had left the table while the waitress was taking orders. I started to think that maybe she was not talking about me. Then I realized that she had to be talking about me. I was the only one at the table who had not yet given a drink order! So, confused, I said, "I would like a water with lemon." The waitress said, "I will be back in a minute to take your order."

So, of course, our conversation turned to things like, "OK, that was strange." I asked the others at the table if the waitress was talking about me when she said to my friend, "What would she like to drink?" They all said, "Oh yeah, she was talking about you." Then, a few minutes later, the waitress came back to serve our drinks and take our lunch orders. She went around the table. Then, when I was the only one left, she again looked at my friend across the table and said, "What would she like to eat?" I was ready this time! Before she finished the sentence, I blurted out, "I would like the grilled chicken sandwich." I said it with confidence so that just maybe the waitress would acknowledge my presence. No such luck! She said, "I will be back shortly with your order." I thought: *What a strange experience.* I had never experienced anything like that. Maybe she was just having a bad day. While I was frustrated and confused, I dismissed it as another weird situation. Well, if only I could say it was a one-time event. I wish I could say that nothing like that lunch experience ever happened again. Unfortunately, I cannot make that statement. Not only did that experience happen again, it continued—and continues—to occur frequently. There are not adequate words to describe how degrading and belittling it feels to be treated as though you are invisible. There was no quicker way during those college years for me to lose self-respect than to be treated as if I was invisible. I interpreted those situations as: This person does not believe I am human and have an equal part in the conversation. Therefore I must not be good enough.

> THERE ARE NOT ADEQUATE WORDS TO DESCRIBE HOW DEGRADING AND BELITTLING IT FEELS TO BE TREATED AS THOUGH YOU ARE INVISIBLE.

Being treated as an invisible person happens to me as a person who is blind, and it also happens to people who are labeled as "other." In countless conversations I have had with people who are considered different, we share stories of the times when we were treated as though we were invisible. So how do we respond to those dehumanizing moments? Do we believe the message that we are not worthy to be considered an equal? Absolutely not! Do we respond in anger and frustration as we lash out at the person? No! What do we do? We give ourselves space to feel the deep level of sadness, anger, and frustration. Then we turn to those people we trust the most. And what do those people say about us? They say that we are fully human. They say through their words and actions that we are worthy and equal human beings.

We also have to turn to look within ourselves. We have to remind ourselves that we are indeed human beings who deserve respect and equality. Yes, there are aspects of our lives that label us as different, and yes, we are worthy of being fully human. Often it is extremely difficult to believe that we deserve the same respect as other people. It is easy to internalize the feeling of being invisible and tell ourselves we do not matter. Changing our thought patterns takes incredible grit. Choosing to have courage, strength, and tenacity is hard work. We have to choose each moment of the day to live with grit so we will believe, deeply within ourselves, that we are respectable human beings.

> BEING ABLE TO NORMALIZE THE NEW REALITY GIVES HOPE AND ENCOURAGEMENT. KNOWING THAT WE ARE NOT THE ONLY ONES GOING THROUGH OUR PARTICULAR DIFFICULTY OR ADVERSITY PROVIDES INCREDIBLE COMFORT.

Transitioning from surviving adversity and trauma to living in a new reality is hard and exhausting—and yet also healing and empowering. Moving from swimming against the ocean current with a life jacket to sitting in the boat is scary and also takes courage. Experiencing the acceptance and affirmation from other people is strengthening beyond words. Being able to normalize the new reality gives hope and encouragement. Knowing that we are not the only ones going through our particular difficulty or adversity provides incredible comfort. We receive grit from other people, a gift that allows us to continue living life. In the midst of receiving acceptance and confidence in our new normal, we also experience degrading, dehumanizing, and belittling words and actions that can leave us feeling less than worthy humans. The harmful words and actions can cause us to believe that we are less than equal. We can start to absorb and believe the negative thoughts and actions. So how do we make sure we stay within the boat rather than jump back in the water and swim against the current? Once again, it all comes down to those two words: grit and gratitude. Adjusting to the new normal requires each of us receiving, and living into, the actions of courage, endurance, and determination shown to us by those who love us and believe that we are worthy. Moving forward in the new normal also means that we have to display grit within ourselves. We have to choose to accept the hurtful comments and actions of others and yet know that we are still humans who deserve respect. Rather than allowing the words and actions to control our perceptions, we have to decide to trust in our courage and strength.

I SUGGEST KEEPING A GRATITUDE JOURNAL, REFLECTING ON ACTIONS OF THANKFULNESS THROUGHOUT THE DAY, AND EXPRESSING OUR GRATITUDE TO OTHER PEOPLE.

Grit is required as we adjust to the new normal. Equally important is gratitude. Words and actions of gratefulness are just as important as we live into our new reality. Being aware of positive people and events provides a deep sense of stability. Focusing on the gifts that carry us through the difficult transitions will help us know just how much goodness surrounds our lives. I suggest keeping a gratitude journal, reflecting on actions of thankfulness throughout the day, and expressing our gratitude to other people. These are all ways we can incorporate gratitude into our daily lives. While it is easy to get trapped in many negative circumstances, a vital part of healing and adjusting is being grateful. Adjusting to adversity is exhausting and difficult, and yet there are still countless moments of gratitude and appreciation we can turn to that provide healing. Choosing to display the balance of courage and strength, as well as thankfulness and gratefulness, allows each of us to live into the new normal in our lives.

Chapter 7

Choosing to Pursue Goals

The new normal can feel both uncomfortable and empowering at the same time. Transitioning to our new reality is often awkward as we figure out how to navigate the new landscape of life. But the time of adjusting is also healing as we gain confidence and strength. During my college years it was extremely important that I was part of an environment that could teach me and show me helpful resources as I adapted to life without sight. After four years at Arizona State University, I had the confidence I needed to be able to advocate for myself. And then life reaches a point when our new normal is not so new anymore. We are now living in the reality of our new set of circumstances in life. We have gone through that first new season of life; the initial time of adjusting and adapting to our new reality is over. We have experienced the first round of growing pains as we struggle to be comfortable in our new place in life.

Does all this mean we will never grieve what we have lost? Does it mean the grieving is forever behind us? It does not. I learned a powerful lesson regarding this that gave me courage—and continues to do so to this day. One day I was in the office of my disability coordinator, Terri. She was going through all the different accommodations I needed. After a long discussion Terri sat back in her chair and said, "Laura, I want to tell you one more thing." I calmly said, "OK. What is that?" I was not at all expecting the words she would deliver next, a piece of advice I will hold onto, and tightly, forever. "Laura, you have gone through the initial process of grieving your vision," she said. "I just want you to know that you will continue to grieve forever. As you come to each new stage in your life you will grieve that you do not have your vision." Sitting in Terri's office as an 18-year-old who was just starting college, I could not fully understand the magnitude of this wisdom. However, I slowly realized this simple truth as I experienced the four years of college and the years that would follow. How true it is that we initially grieve as we struggle with our new normal. Then, as we gain courage and strength, we move forward. We are empowered even as we continue to grieve.

> HOW TRUE IT IS THAT WE INITIALLY GRIEVE AS WE STRUGGLE WITH OUR NEW NORMAL. THEN, AS WE GAIN COURAGE AND STRENGTH, WE MOVE FORWARD. WE ARE EMPOWERED EVEN AS WE CONTINUE TO GRIEVE.

* * * * * * *

After graduating from Arizona State, I started a masters of divinity program at Princeton Theological Seminary. I decided to pursue the profession of being a clergy who works with people experiencing trauma and loss. My professional goal was to provide spiritual support to individuals and families going through difficult circumstances. Why was I passionate about providing spiritual support in this way? I mean, should that not have been the last career in the world I would choose? I didn't grow up thinking or even dreaming that I would one day be a clergy. The profession was never on my radar. So why did I choose to get my masters of divinity? The combination of my strengths and passion in helping people, as well as my life experiences, compelled me to pursue the role of a clergy. Going through the horrible traumatizing time of my vision decreasing and adapting to life without sight, I experienced the powerful Spirit of God. Yes, I spent countless nights telling God I could not do life without sight. Yes, I was mad and angry that God had not healed me instantly. But, along with those emotions of sadness and anger, I was and continue to be forever changed by the love of God. The love, power, and strength of God came through family, friends, community, and com-

I EXPERIENCED THE POWERFUL SPIRIT OF GOD. YES, I SPENT COUNTLESS NIGHTS TELLING GOD I COULD NOT DO LIFE WITHOUT SIGHT. YES, I WAS MAD AND ANGRY THAT GOD HAD NOT HEALED ME INSTANTLY.

plete strangers. There are countless times when I receive the experience of God being with me through the pain and difficulty and God, at the same time, empowering me to move forward with purpose and meaning. Each story I have shared in this book is an example of powerful encounters with the loving Spirit who created each of our lives. So I was passionate about choosing a profession that would allow me to teach about and share the love of God that is present in our lives regardless of the circumstances.

There was one major difference in going to Arizona State University compared with Princeton Theological Seminary. No, I am not talking about the weather change from perfect, sunny days to cold, snowy days, although that was a major change, and it did require an entirely new wardrobe! I am referring to the fact that at Arizona State University I was not the first student who was blind, as I have said, nor was I the only blind student on campus. At Princeton Theological Seminary, I was going to be the first student in the two hundred-year history of the school who would be blind. Once I was accepted to the school I received a powerful gift. Both the president and the administration said to me, "We do not know what accommodations you need. We know that we are not equipped for people who are blind. You tell us the resources that you need, and we will make it happen." Wow! I was incredibly grateful. I was most thankful that they were honest and open about the fact they were not prepared for blind students. I was even more grateful for their willingness to work with me. I was deeply appreciative that they were willing to grow and change so that Princeton would be a school that is accessible for all people. You know those moments when we receive gifts we are not expecting? These are the gifts that make life much easier and less exhausting. Well, I experienced one of those surprising gifts in the words and actions of the school president and administration. So for the six months before I started graduate school, I worked closely with the administration so that we were both prepared and equipped.

One day I was speaking with an administrator about getting my textbooks in electronic format. At the end of the conversation he said, "Laura, I want to let you know that this is not going to be a bed of roses, but we will work together and we will make it happen." Again, this was one of those moments when I would receive a piece of wisdom that would stay with me forever. The administrator was honestly saying that it was not going to be smooth as the school learned how to work with me and as I learned how to be part of a school that was not already equipped for students with disabilities. While he said it would not be anything close to easy, he clearly was telling me that the school and I would work together to make it a successful experience for both the school and myself. The statement was just what I needed to hear! No, it was not going to be perfect as I learned to communicate my needs and as the school learned to adapt. But yes, it was going to be doable because we were all willing to work together.

What a powerful lesson for each of us facing challenges and adversity. Working through the obstacles in our lives is never going to be a bed of roses. Overcoming challenges will never be smooth and easy. Instead, life can feel like a bed of thorns. Learning how to navigate through the painful difficulties takes courage and determination. Courage is required to acknowledge the difficult situation. Courage is also required for the actions that allow us to move forward. Equally as important as courage is determination; it takes determination to move through life's bed of thorns. But along with courage and determination, gratitude also is needed to survive the proverbial bed of thorns. Being constantly aware of the people and events that make us thankful empowers us to continue through those most difficult times. Being grateful is like adding fuel to a car. Without fuel, the car goes nowhere. Once the proper fuel is added, the car is able to go places. Gratitude is the fuel that allows our spirits to continue moving through adversity. Without moments of appreciation we get stuck in endless cycles of negativity. It's true—we are not exactly bubbling over with joy and thanksgiving in the midst of challenges. However, we can have moments of deep gratefulness for the people and events that allow us to overcome and move on through the hard times.

I experienced a moment of thankfulness one afternoon about a week after graduate school started. Actually, it wasn't just a moment, it was much longer and deeper than a brief, passing thought of gratitude. After classes I went to check my mail. I had been given a mailbox on the end of a row so I could easily find it. I opened the box, pulled out the mail and I realized one of the letters was in braille. Braille? Who in the world could have written me a braille letter? I could have counted on one hand the people I knew who might send me a letter in braille. So I opened the letter and it read: "Dear Laura, I wanted to send you a piece of mail that you could read immediately. Welcome to PTS. I am excited that you are here. I hope everything is off to a great start. I learned braille a long time ago because a friend of mine was blind. So it has been many years since I have written a letter. Sorry for any mistakes. Again, welcome to campus! With love, Dr. Brown."[7]

> I INSTANTLY FELT LIKE THE KID WHO RUNS AROUND JUMPING UP AND DOWN SHOWING EVERYONE HER NEW TOY.

I instantly felt like the kid who runs around jumping up and down showing everyone her new toy. I wanted to both wave my letter around, screaming, "Look what I got!" and I wanted to stand there speechless at the same time. Dr. Brown was not one of my professors that first semester. I had met her, but we had not worked together as I prepared to start the masters program. She wrote a letter to me simply because she wanted to welcome me. Dr. Brown said through her words and actions: I want you to feel welcomed! I want you to feel that you matter here. I want you to be able to open a piece of mail and quickly read it like everyone else. What a gift; one that cannot be bought! What a true gift that I will never forget. In the moment after reading the letter, I was deeply grateful. I was deeply appreciative of the time Dr. Brown took from her busy schedule to write and send me a letter.

All afternoon as I thought about that letter, I was grateful. It was like I had received a boost of energy. Thinking about the letter made me stop and reflect on the past six months. I was deeply thankful for the president, administration, chaplain, professors, and so many different staff members who worked with me in the months before that fall semester started. I cannot even begin to list all the accommodations that were made so I could start school just like all the other students. Some of the accommodations included assigning a library staff member to help get and produce my textbooks in electronic format, installing an audible signal at a crosswalk, buying a screen reader for a computer in the computer lab, and working with the cafeteria staff so I could easily receive my food. Yes, I was nervous and even exhausted during that first week of classes. I was overwhelmed. But even in the midst of feeling overwhelmed, I was grateful. What a gift so many people had been to me to make it possible to start my masters program.

YES, I WAS NERVOUS AND EVEN EXHAUSTED DURING THAT FIRST WEEK OF CLASSES. I WAS OVERWHELMED. BUT EVEN IN THE MIDST OF FEELING OVERWHELMED, I WAS GRATEFUL.

Words cannot describe what it is like when we receive gifts like the braille letter or the actions shown me by the administration and staff. You know those gifts that say: *You matter.*

You are worthy. It is those gifts that give us courage to continue living out our meaning and purpose. Receiving such gifts
from others reminds us of the incredible value of our lives
regardless of the ways we have been labeled.

During the time that I worked with the administration and
staff to prepare for my program, I gained a huge amount of
confidence. Transitioning from a school equipped for people
with disabilities to a school with limited experience in this
area gave me the opportunity to advocate for myself. I had to
clearly know my needs. I had to know how to communicate
those needs. I had to know what accommodations were best. I
had to be willing to problem-solve and think quickly to come
up with solutions. I also had to be willing to say, "Here is a
need that I have and let's brainstorm to figure out an answer."
Like any other learning experience, it was not smooth. There
were days I was so fearful and anxious. I was ready to say that
I was not going to graduate from the school. I told myself that
it was just too hard and too much work to prepare. I was worn
out and classes had not even started!

I remember one day when I announced to my parents, "By
the way, I do not have the strength to do this whole advocat-
ing-for-yourself thing. It is just too hard." How did they respond? "Oh, that is OK. Just give up." Or did they respond,
"Just get over it and keep going!" No! They said, "Yes, it is unbelievably exhausting. Take it in small parts at a time and you
will get through it and everything will come together." Well,
their answer was not what I wanted to hear, but it was true.
Learning how to advocate for our needs can be overwhelming. We have to take life part by part. It is like putting together
a puzzle. The puzzle is not put together by just laying down
one big piece and then the puzzle is complete. Instead, it requires putting down one piece of the puzzle at a time. So, too,
learning how to advocate for ourselves is accomplished part

by part.

While learning to advocate for myself made me fearful and anxious, I also gained confidence with each piece of the puzzle that was securely placed. What courage it gave me when I was able to communicate my needs and work with others so that those needs were met. Living in our present reality in the midst of struggles and difficulties, it is crucial that we are able to serve as our own advocates. We do not always need the perfect solution. We do, however, have to be open and patient as we seek to advocate for ourselves.

I was gaining confidence in learning to advocate for myself. I was also growing and healing spiritually. You know those times in our lives when someone we trust and respect makes a recommendation and we follow through just because we trust that person's wisdom? Well, after my first semester, I was meeting with one of my mentors when I was home. During the conversation he said to me, "So, Laura, PTS offers spiritual direction to their students, right?" I answered, "Yes, I know they do." He then asked me if I was in spiritual direction. I told him I had heard of it, but I was not.

"Well, Laura," he said. "Start it as soon as you can."

Once I was back at school I got information about spiritual direction and scheduled my first appointment. At my first session the spiritual director said, "Have you had spiritual direction before?" I laughed and said, "Oh no. I really have no clue what this is. I am just here because a mentor told me that I needed to receive spiritual direction. So here I am!" I had no clue that I was starting a path of incredible spiritual healing. Sitting there in the first session, I could not have dreamed of the powerful ways that my life would be strengthened and changed.

What is spiritual direction? The program creates the space for individuals or groups to explore the spiritual parts of

NOW, LET ME ASSURE YOU THAT SITTING IN SILENCE IS NOT EASY FOR AN EXTROVERTED SOUTHERN GIRL! MY FAMILY AND FRIENDS WILL QUICKLY ATTEST THAT I'M ALWAYS TALKING AND NEVER SILENT!

their lives. It also creates the space for people to be aware of the holy in the everyday life. Spiritual direction is practiced in many different religions. For me, spiritual direction gave me the space to talk about my relationship with God and reflect on the ways God is present in my life. Most importantly was the time my spiritual director and I spent in silence listening to the living Spirit and then talking about what came up for me in the silent reflection. Now, let me assure you that sitting in silence is not easy for an extroverted Southern girl! My family and friends will quickly attest that I'm always talking and never silent! So first, sitting still and in silence is not natural for me! As my spiritual director and I met once a month until I graduated, the time was incredibly healing. Words cannot describe how the time changed my spirit.

There is one major shift and source of healing that took place, and it can be described in one word: identity. My spiritual identity was healed and strengthened. Being raised in a Christian home and attending church each Sunday gave me a strong foundation. I knew Scripture, I knew how to pray, I knew how to be part of the actions of justice through serving, and I trusted the God who created me. I strongly experienced the presence of God in my life. Throughout the trauma of becoming blind, I desperately cried out to God, telling God that I could not do life without sight. I wrestled and bargained with God. My relationship became one of dependence as I needed strength, hope, and courage from God. I learned the value and gift of praying to God for anything I needed, large or small. One minute I would pray when I dropped something on the floor and could not find it, while another time I would be praying for God to give me the strength to get up out of bed and face the day. Through the horrible time of adjusting to blindness, I learned about the immeasurable love and power of God's Spirit that sustains us regardless of the situation.

Why was the identity piece so huge for me? Each session gave me the opportunity to sit in silence listening to the Spirit of God. I was not asking God for anything. I was not wrestling and bargaining with God. I was simply and powerfully sitting in the holy presence of God's living Spirit. As the past years had been difficult adjusting to life without sight, I now had the space and opportunity to be still and understand who I am. First, I am a normal child from the southeastern part of the United States. Then, I am a disabled person. In many ways I felt like a normal human being while in many other ways I felt totally disabled and different. Some people label me as amazing because I get out of bed in the morning. Some people label me as disabled while others say that I am *differently abled.* Some people talk louder and slower to me while others treat me as if I am invisible. Yet others treat me as a full human, acknowledging that I have a disability and need help. Who in the world am I? If my identity is based on how others perceive me, my identity will change, literally, every second. Then where is my identity? Through the spiritual foundation that was created for me, I was able to sit in each spiritual direction session and know my true, lasting identity. I am a beloved child of God. My identity is rooted and established in the fact that I am a be-

> SOME PEOPLE LABEL ME AS DISABLED WHILE OTHERS SAY THAT I AM *DIFFERENTLY ABLED.*

loved creation of the creator of the universe. The living Spirit does not label me as blind, different, or disabled. I am equally as valuable as all other humans created. Yes, I am a beloved child of God and yes, each person created is a beloved child of God.

As humans we experience countless situations and circumstances that cause us to question our identity. This can be confusing or hurtful. So many of us ask the questions: *Who am I? What is my identity?* But we are each given a specific identity by God. What a gift that we can know our true identity regardless of the other identities we have been given. We are each beloved children of the creator. We are each equally created and loved by the living Spirit of God. What healing and strength comes from the gift of knowing our true, lasting identity does not change with circumstances or time.

As I became aware of my identity as a beloved child of God, did I have an earth-shattering transformation? Absolutely not! The change was a slow and yet deep transformation in my spirit. It was a deep change I became aware of, started to live into, and will forever trust. I trust the promise that my true, lasting identity is that I am a beloved child of God. Does the Spirit of God know I am blind? Does the living Spirit know my needs? Does the Spirit know that I need incredible strength, courage, and endurance? The answer to all these questions is: absolutely! The promise that we are each equal, beloved children of God does not take away from the fact that the spirit knows our unique circumstances and situations. Rather, we have the promise that within our diversity and differences we are each beloved creations of God. What courage, strength, and determination comes from knowing who we are in our spirit when we understand that spirit has been given to us by God. Going through adversity and adjusting to life after adversity is much easier when we have the strong foundation of knowing that we are each beloved creations.

As I received healing for my spirit through spiritual direction, I also received healing through learning mindfulness. Similar to spiritual direction, I signed up for a workshop on mindfulness only because a friend recommended that I go. Again, I had no clue what it was, and I also had no idea how much it would help me in day-to-day life. Mindfulness is being aware of the present moment. Mindfulness also includes acknowledging one's thoughts and feelings. I am a professional at having fearful thoughts and then experiencing those fears growing exponentially. Having fear about starting grad school is a perfect example. I was so fearful about the effort it would take to make sure everything was accessible. My fearful thoughts took on a life of their own and I seriously considered not even starting the program. Through learning the practice of mindfulness, I learned how to acknowledge fearful thoughts and then let the thoughts go. Rather than holding tightly to the thoughts, as though they were truth, I learned that I could have these thoughts and then let them go. Mindfulness also taught me another valuable lesson. I would start to feel fearful, anxious, angry, or sad and try to stop those feelings.

WHAT HAPPENS WHEN WE TRY TO PUSH AWAY A THOUGHT? IT GROWS, AND WE KEEP THINKING ABOUT WHAT WE ARE TRYING NOT TO THINK ABOUT!

I would push the feelings away. A typical conversation in my mind went something like this: *I am so anxious about starting grad school. I cannot do this. I cannot do this. No, I cannot be anxious. If I keep up these thoughts, I will be extremely nervous.* Well, what happens when we try to push away a thought? It grows, and we keep thinking about what we are trying not to think about! What a horrible cycle! Mindfulness taught me that I can acknowledge and feel the emotions rather than putting exhausting effort into trying to keep the emotions away.

During times of trauma and throughout the time that we are adjusting to the new normal, it is extremely easy to get caught up in the cycle of harmful thoughts and feelings. Of course, we are going to feel such a range of emotions as we adjust and move forward in the midst of challenges. How normal and healthy it is to allow ourselves to feel and experience these thoughts and feelings. The problem comes when the harmful thoughts and feelings become our normal thought patterns. Mindfulness is a powerful tool and resource that can help us move from a place of negativity to a place where we can acknowledge our thoughts and feelings and choose to move forward with courage and strength.

Just as I received wisdom when I sat in the office of my mentor and he told me to start spiritual direction, I experienced an additional gift of wisdom sitting in another office. As part of the masters program we were required to do different field education placements. During the summer between the second and third year of the program, I was a summer intern at Princeton United Methodist Church. The internship was complete and I was sitting in the office of the senior pastor for my final evaluation. We went through all the different ways I had been involved in the church. We talked about the different experiences I was able to have in this professional clergy role. After telling me about the various strengths I displayed through the summer, Jana said, "So, there is one area that I want you to work on." I thought, *Oh, this will be easy since she is only going to give me one area!* Well, I was totally wrong. Easy? What was I thinking? She went on to say, "Laura, I want you to work on not resisting. Each time I gave you a new task of leadership or responsibility, your first reaction was to resist. You put time and energy into resisting the new responsibility.

Then you did what you needed to do to fulfill the task, and it all worked out great."[8]

You know those moments when someone says something to you that is so true and right on target? Well, I had one of those moments sitting in this final evaluation. I knew exactly what Jana was talking about. She did not need to say more. One example was when I was given the task of creating and leading a summer Bible study. I sat in her office telling her lots of good reasons why I should not be the one to lead the study. I gave plenty of suggestions of other leadership roles I could handle instead of leading a study. Why did I resist? Why did I spend so much energy holding back from trying the new leadership position? Several reasons. I resisted because I was exhausted by the thought of learning the new leadership role as well as figuring out how to adapt so I could perform the leadership role. I was fearful because of questions like: Can I do this? Will I fail? Will my blindness stop me from succeeding in the position? Maybe it has nothing to do with my blindness, I told myself; maybe it's more of an issue that this is a role I cannot adequately perform. These and other questions raced through my mind uncontrollably. The fear of the new situation caused me to resist. And I was not consciously aware I was resisting! I was not exactly thinking of how could I resist in this situation. Rather, it took Jana's strength to point out the fact that I was actively resisting.

As Jana and I talked about it more and as I thought back over each new leadership role, I learned a valuable lesson. The energy it takes to resist and hold back from moving forward is much more exhausting and fear-inducing than actually choosing to embrace a situation. The paralyzing, fearful questions of doubt hold us back and prevent us from using our strengths and gifts. Incredible grit is required to move forward in new situations. Courage, determination, and tenacity are needed so we can embrace the new situation regardless of the challenges. Resisting can feel more comfortable because it does not require us to move forward in unfamiliar territory in which we do not know the outcome. However, choosing to let go of resistance is freeing and empowering. What a gift we each receive when we choose courage and perseverance over withholding and resisting.

Adjusting to the new normal is hard, exhausting. Gaining confidence in our new reality is fearful and overwhelming. As we move through the experiences that require incredible amounts of strength, courage, and endurance, there are also moments of joy, laughter, and thanksgiving. The friendships I made while in graduate school were incredible gifts! I knew by the end of the first week of school that I was going to love graduate school. Why? It wasn't exactly because of the thousand academic reading assignments! Although the reading was interesting, it was more because, during that first week, I spent one day with five other people I had just met and we were taking the train from Princeton to New York City! I knew then that I was going to like this whole masters of divinity program! The fun times, like taking trips into the city, as well as being with friends going to our favorite restaurants, ice cream shops, or shopping, were all sources of fun and recreation that kept me balanced with all the hard work of adapting and completing the academic work.

During the times of living into a new normal and adjusting to our new reality, life can be stressful and intense as we constantly work to adapt and be comfortable in our own skin. As much as our lives require actions of courage and tenacity, we also need times when we can have fun, relax, and laugh. The healing power of laughter is incredible. Learning to laugh at ourselves is healing and healthy. The second year of graduate school I was taking a class in preaching. The class required that we each preach several sermons. The day arrived when I was going to preach my first sermon for the class. About ten students, the professor, and I were sitting in a small classroom. It was my turn at the podium. Of course, I was so nervous and had practiced the sermon about one hundred times. I started, and it was going as I had prepared and planned. Then, toward the middle, I blanked out. I froze. I forgot, in that moment, what my next part was going to be. So, without missing a beat, I quickly glanced down at the podium, where most people would have laid their notes. It was just a normal glance down to "read my notes" and then continue on. For most people that is a great idea, what nearly anyone needs to do in that moment. There is only one problem. I am blind! I did not have any notes on the podium, and if I did they would be in braille, so I would not be looking down! I collected my thoughts, continued my preaching, and finished the sermon. During the time of feedback, the professor said, "I want to start with one question. What was that quick glance down at the podium when you hesitated?" I burst out laughing and said, "Great question! I have no clue!" Of course, I knew in that moment that looking down as if I was reading my notes was not going to help me. I just had to laugh at myself.

FOR MOST PEOPLE THAT IS A GREAT IDEA, WHAT NEARLY ANYONE NEEDS TO DO IN THAT MOMENT. THERE IS ONLY ONE PROBLEM. I AM BLIND!

Getting to know and becoming friends with international students at graduate school was such a source of joy. Learning about different cultures and getting to know the international students as friends was a gift. We spent hours laughing as well as supporting each other. Yes, we had many cultural differences, and we had many similarities. What a gift it was to learn from each other. During the first fall semester I had a class every Tuesday for several hours. In this class I got to know Son-yong. She was only going to be at seminary for a year. A few weeks into the class we were walking out together. Once we got to Son-yong's dorm she kept walking with me. As we came to the street, she crossed it with me and said, "Laura, I want to walk back with you to your apartment." My immediate thought was, *Oh, she totally thinks that I cannot walk the next few blocks by myself. Oh please!* As I was having this thought, Son-yong said to me, "I know you Americans want to be independent. I know you can walk back to your apartment by yourself. I just want to spend more time talking to you as my friend." So was my immediate thought wrong or what? What a powerful lesson I learned from Son-yong that day. During the first week of orientation we had been told that many of the friendships we would make throughout the program would be friendships for life. Indeed, I developed many close friendships that have continued after graduate school and will continue forever. What a gift friends are as we adjust to our new normal. The friendships are not based on the fact that we are striving to adjust to our new reality. Rather, the friendships are based on other aspects of our lives that connect us with other people.

Incredible perseverance and endurance is required as we adjust to life despite adversities and struggles. Life in the new normal requires the grit that we display as well as the grit shown by our family, friends, and community. Deep gratitude is felt when we can reflect on our lives and notice the countless actions of grit that surround our lives.

I had one of those moments of deep gratitude on graduation day. It was a beautiful, sunny Saturday in late May and my graduating class was sitting in the Princeton Chapel for our ceremony. After each of us walked across the stage to receive our diploma, the dean of Student Life said, "Now we have one more diploma to give." She paused, then added, "This degree goes to an individual who was faithful to attend every single class, but slept through each class. On behalf of Princeton Theological Seminary, we give the first ever masters of dogmatics to Jira Bratton." Princeton is known worldwide for its emphasis on the famous theologian Karl Barth. Barth wrote the church dogmatics, a collection of hundreds of volumes of books that outline his theology and teaching. Since the school is the top center in the world for scholars to study church dogmatics, how appropriate it was to give my guide dog a masters in dogmatics! Just a little Ivy League humor!

THE SCHOOL PRESIDENT AND ADMINISTRATION CHOOSING TO GIVE JIRA AN OFFICIAL MASTERS DEGREE COMPLETELY SUMS UP THE GRIT THE SCHOOL DISPLAYED FOR ME THROUGHOUT THE THREE YEARS.

To say that I was shocked and speechless when the dean announced this "masters degree" is an understatement. So the chaplain and I walked back to the stage and the president handed me a second diploma tube, one identical to those everyone else had received. The administration had put a ribbon around the tube so I could tie it around Jira's neck. Of course, as soon as I did, Jira shook it off. I reached down, picked up her diploma, and we walked across the stage. Jira's diploma is just as official as those of the rest of the students! It is complete with her name, the masters of dogmatics degree, and the school seal. Needless to say, it is framed and hangs beside my diploma today. The school president and administration choosing to give Jira an official masters degree completely sums up the grit the school displayed for me throughout the three years. There, on graduation day, surrounded by my family and friends, I was grateful that I was not struggling to live into my new normal alone. Rather, I felt the support of family, friends, and community.

Overcoming life's traumas and adversities are not tasks that should be undertaken alone. Rather, adjusting and living in our new normal takes the needed courage of those around us.

Chapter 8

Living into Strengths and Gifts

I chose to pursue a masters of divinity degree because of my passion to provide support to people in times of crisis and trauma. Yes, my decision was based on the fact that I had been through the trauma of becoming blind. Having experienced the unconditional love from God that came through my family, friends, community, and complete strangers, I had to spend my life also sharing the hope and love of the loving Spirit that flows between each of our lives regardless of our circumstances. But there was another major factor that led to my decision: my strengths and gifts were the other major component. I always knew that I would have a career in the helping profession. Even as a small child, both children and adults would start talking to me, sharing all of their struggles. Complete strangers would just pour out their life stories to me. So it became clear my strengths were to actively listen, offer compassion, and be a supportive presence. I also quickly realized what professions I would not pursue and what were not my strengths and gifts. For example, I do not have any strengths in the field of music. The few years that I took piano lessons quickly showed me that I did not need to pursue music! You know your gifting in an area is pretty bad when your grandmother says to a friend, "Oh, Laura has many gifts, but music is not one of them." And my grandmother was correct!

When we are confronted with adversity and obstacles, whether they be acute situations or long-term events, it is easy to allow the difficulty to define us. We can get caught up in the mind-set that our whole lives are centered on the trauma. We forget that we are still human beings with gifts and purpose. Once we have initially worked through our grief and loss, it can still be difficult to remember and know that we all have strengths. We are more than simply our difficulties. Choosing to have grit moment by moment is required to remind ourselves that the adversity does not have to define us. Yes, the difficulties and obstacles absolutely affect our lives, and deeply. Our lives often must drastically change because of obstacles. But as we make these major changes, we find we are defined by more than just the adversity. We are each humans who are worthy of and deserve equal respect.

Being in graduate school preparing for my professional career gave me the perfect opportunity to live into my strengths and gifts. As I had already gone through the initial grieving process, I was at a point where I could now focus on the other

> WE CAN GET CAUGHT UP IN THE MIND-SET THAT OUR WHOLE LIVES ARE CENTERED ON THE TRAUMA. WE FORGET THAT WE ARE STILL HUMAN BEINGS WITH GIFTS AND PURPOSE.

parts of my life. I could focus on growing into my professional strengths.

* * * * * * *

After my first year of graduate school I had a summer internship. Five other students and I had one unit of clinical pastoral education; we were chaplain interns at JFK Medical Center in Edison, New Jersey. The internship was an incredible opportunity for me to live into my professional role. Before I started, my supervisor and I worked together to make sure the job was accessible for me. I wanted to be able to start and focus on the work like everyone else. One particular accommodation that I received was having access to a hospital laptop with a screen reader. Having a laptop would allow me to participate in classes just like everyone else since I could then follow along with the handouts. I could also use the laptop for patient notes and charting. I was most grateful for the accommodation and I was equally thankful for my supervisor's next action. Dr. Griesel did not just provide a laptop for me, she provided a laptop for each of the other students in the group. Dr. Griesel realized a laptop would greatly assist me, but she also realized that the other students in the group would also benefit from a laptop. Dr. Griesel met a need that I had but also provided the same resource for the other class students. She showed me through her actions that she treated me as an equal. She was not treating me differently. She was going to provide for every accommodation I needed while also holding me to the same standards as others.

Living into our strengths and gifts requires moment to moment courage. What a huge gift we receive when others come alongside us and value our gifts. How empowering it is to be treated as an equal. Living into our new normal, using our gifts and strengths, requires both grit within ourselves and the grit of other people.

The first week of the internship I jumped right back into that anxious, fearful mind-set. My mind was racing with thoughts such as: *How will I do this? There is no way I can do this. What was I thinking? Maybe I could just quit now and say, "Oh, I thought the internship would work out, but it is not."* My heart was pounding faster and faster and I had that horrible feeling in the pit of my stomach. The anxiety was quickly increasing in my mind and body. I wanted to walk away and quit—no, actually I wanted to run far away and quit! It seemed easier to give up and not try rather than put the effort into adapting. As my mind raced with anxious thoughts and my heart continued to pound faster and faster, I remembered the wisdom I had received from my disability coordinator in college. At each new stage I arrived at in life, I would grieve my vision loss. I would grieve that I did not have vision and would again have to adapt to the new situation and circumstances. Indeed, here I was at a new point in my life. I had adapted and adjusted to life as a blind student. Now I had to adjust to being a professional, and one with a disability. Remember how my brother told me, at certain times, that we would drop back and punt? Well, this was one of those drop-back-and-punt moments. With the grit of those around me and with courage

> AS MY MIND RACED WITH ANXIOUS THOUGHTS AND MY HEART CONTINUED TO POUND FASTER AND FASTER, I REMEMBERED THE WISDOM I HAD RECEIVED FROM MY DISABILITY COORDINATOR IN COLLEGE. AT EACH NEW STAGE THAT I ARRIVED AT IN LIFE, I WOULD GRIEVE MY VISION LOSS.

within myself, I could indeed adapt and enter the professional world. Was the adjustment going to be easy and quick? No! But it was absolutely going to be worth the time and effort.

Those times in our lives when we get overwhelmed by anxiety and fear are like moments of climbing a steep mountain. After a short distance up the mountain, when it starts to get hard and difficult, it seems easier, even better, to just turn around and go back to the mountain base. The work and effort to hike to the top seems impossible. Yet we know that getting to the top is what is best for us and where we need to be. So what do we do? Do we sprint up the mountain with no effort or little work? Do we just decide that we want to be at the top and magically find ourselves at the summit? It just doesn't work that way. Hiking up a steep and treacherous mountain requires intentional preparation as well as physical endurance for a long period of time. As we hike up a mountain we will get exhausted and have to stop and rest. We will also have to take breaks for water and food. Sometimes we will be so hot we think we are facing serious heat exhaustion. At other points in the hike the wind will whip up, the temperatures will drop, and we will be freezing. The hike will not be simple or quick, yet getting to the summit is more than worth it.

Working through anxiety and fear is like hiking up the mountain—it is hard and exhausting. Yet it is exactly what is required so we are not controlled by our anxieties and fears. Rather, we are free to use our gifts and talents. We are free to live a life of purpose and meaning. Working through the anxiety and fear means that we give ourselves the space to feel the difficult feelings, decide to let those feelings go, and then choose to have courage and endurance. We also depend on those around us and our spiritual resources to help us move through the anxieties and fears. How crucial it is for us to remember that we are not alone in this thing called life. Rather, we are surrounded by the support and love of others.

I was overwhelmed with anxieties and fears that first week of the chaplain internship. I found ways to work through them, but those worries did not then suddenly evaporate and leave me only feeling peace and hope. Rather, working through my feelings took time and courage. I had to choose to live moment by moment. I gained confidence each time I chose to move forward rather than staying in my anxious thoughts. And it greatly helped knowing that my supervisor and many others around me believed in my abilities. I also gained confidence as I provided pastoral care to patients.

One day, about halfway through the internship, I was called to visit a patient on the oncology unit. David was in his sixties and hospitalized for low blood counts after receiving chemotherapy. A few moments into our conversation David said, "Chaplain, God does not love me. There is no way that God could love me. I just know it." Then, without giving me a chance to say anything, David said, "God does not love me because of all the things in my life I have done. Listen to what I have done." He went on for a few minutes, listing all of the reasons God could not love him. Once he was through, I said, "David, you have mentioned that you have children. Tell me more about each of your children." So David started telling me their names, ages, where they lived, and their professions. Then I asked David a simple question. "So, tell me what they could do so that you would stop loving them." Without hesitating, David quickly said, "Oh chaplain, I will always love my children. They are my children and I love them to death. There is nothing that they can do that would cause me to stop loving them." Once David finished that answer, I said, "Oh really? So there is nothing?" "Yes. Yes! I mean it, chaplain. I will always love them." After a moment I said, "So, David, if you can and will love your children no matter what they do, how do you think the God who created you thinks about you? If there are no actions that your children can do that will cause you to stop loving them, what actions could you do that would make the God who created you stop loving you?" The room went silent. David and I sat there for the next few minutes without a word being said. Then, in a quiet voice, he said, "So, you think God loves me? You think I am really worthy of God's love?" I confidently said, "Absolutely. You are worthy of God's love." After a few more moments of silence, the nurse came in David's room to take his vitals and give him fluids. So I told David to think about our conversation, and that I would be back to visit him. Over the next few days David and I were able to continue our conversation as he worked hard to receive the truth that God loves him and that he is worthy of God's love.

Observing the changes in David throughout our conversations, and being able to listen and support him, as well as other patient interactions, taught me a valuable lesson: I can indeed pursue my professional career. Yes, it will be hard. And there will be times when I am anxious and fearful because I am blind. Sometimes it will feel like I am hiking up the mountain exhausted and ready to quit. Yet I can continue forward with my strengths and gifts.

I am grateful for this internship, which gave me the opportunity to begin the process of living into my professional identity. I am grateful for my supervisor,

I AM ALSO DEEPLY THANKFUL FOR THE OTHER STUDENTS IN MY GROUP WHO HELPED ME WHEN I NEEDED IT, ALL WHILE TREATING ME AS AN EQUAL. HAVING AN ATTITUDE OF GRATEFULNESS HELPS KEEP EACH OF US FOCUSED AS WE LET GO OF OUR ANXIETIES AND FEARS.

who accepted me into the program and worked hard to make the necessary accommodations while also holding me to the same standards. I am also deeply thankful for the other students in my group who helped me when I needed it, all while treating me as an equal. Having an attitude of gratefulness helps keep each of us focused as we let go of our anxieties and fears.

During my final evaluation, my supervisor and I were reflecting on the program. Dr. Griesel said to me, "Laura, I want you to never forget one important fact. Over the internship you have proven that you can do the work. From this point forward, no matter what you face or who you encounter, never forget that you can do the work." She went on to say, "You and I worked together to make the necessary accommodations that you needed. Once the accommodations were in place, you were able to fulfill your role just like everyone else. So Laura, never forget that your blindness does not stop you from your work."[9] I sat across from her not knowing how to respond. I nodded my head, smiled, and said, "Thank you." What a gift I had just received. I was incredibly grateful that Dr. Griesel had spoken these simple words of truth. Dr. Griesel empowered me to continue moving forward. What freedom she gave me to believe and know that my blindness did not define me. Rather, I could live into my strengths and gifts.

As we each experience situations and circumstances that cause us to be anxious and fearful, it seems better in the moment to allow those fears and anxious thoughts to take over and control our lives. Yes, there will be those moments and times when, indeed, our fears do seem to have control over us. But rather than allowing the anxious thoughts to dominate our lives, we can choose to live into grit and gratitude. Even though it is not comfortable, we can choose to have courage, strength, and endurance so that we can freely move beyond these fears. We also need the gift of gratitude. Taking the time to be thankful will empower our lives. Being grateful for the people who support us is encouraging. Hiking up the mountain of life as we live into our purpose takes incredible courage, perseverance, and gratefulness.

* * * * * * *

After completing graduate school, I started a residency in clinical pastoral education; I was a chaplain at the Cleveland Clinic in Cleveland, Ohio. Just as with my chaplain internship, the residency would be a time for me to continually learn and grow into my identity as a professional. I would once again be confronted with deciding if I was going to allow anxiety and fear to paralyze me and stop me, or if I was going to continue to display tenacity and perseverance. Yet again, it was as though I was not far on my journey up the mountain when I felt that, just maybe, the best choice was to run and give up. Thankfully, with the support of my family and friends, I chose to continue hiking upward. As the anxiety and fears would race through my mind, I remembered Dr. Griesel's words: "Over the internship you have proven that you can do the work. From this point forward, no matter what you face or who you encounter, never forget that you can do the work." Each day before work I would use different spiritual resources such as prayer, centering prayer, and meditation to calm my anxious thoughts and fears. Throughout the day I would try to remember mindfulness practices like being aware of the present moment, acknowledging my feelings, and letting the feelings go.

Throughout life, as we experience situations that are extremely difficult and challenging, it is not as simple as saying, "Oh, I am not going to be anxious, therefore I will never have another anxious thought." Instead, moving through the anxiety and fear requires effort and work. Acknowledging those anxious thoughts and letting them go is more like hiking up Mount Everest than hiking a smaller mountain. The upward goal is not only to get rid of the anxiety and fear that we experience in the moment, it is also to develop a mind-set that enables us to live out a life of purpose in which the fearful thoughts do not consume our lives.

Throughout the residency, I had amazing opportunities that allowed me to gain confidence in my professional role. On several of my assigned adult units, I was part of the nurses' and case workers' daily rounds. The first week of the residency I was on one of my adult units introducing myself to the nurse manager as well as the nurses. The nurse manager, Debbie, said, "Laura, come and be part of our rounds. I would like for you to join us and give your input as we go over each patient." I first thought, *Really? You want me there for the expertise that I bring to the table? Seriously?* I was excited. Going on the rounds taught me so much about the role of a chaplain. And I learned another valuable lesson. The nurse manager, nurses, social workers, case managers, and other people who came to the meetings were not interacting with me differently than anyone else. They were not focusing on the fact that I am blind. Rather, they cared that I sat at the table as a professional who was part of the team. Like Dr. Griesel, they showed me through their actions that they valued my gifts and strengths.

They were not treating me less than anyone else. What confidence I received as I grew even more comfortable in my professional role. I realized I needed to let go of the fear of how others might perceive me. I could choose to believe that I had what I needed. I could stop worrying about what others thought of my blindness and know that I was enough.

Am I enough? Is that true? I asked myself that important question frequently. As a person with a disability, it is easy to slip into the mind-set of thinking and believing that I am not enough. When I am treated "less than" or treated as though I am invisible, I can easily fall into this hole. I have had conversations with many other people with disabilities who wondered if they have, or are, *enough*. In fact, the question *Am I enough?* is not only a struggle for people with disabilities. The question is one that everyone wrestles with in some way. I have had countless conversations, both professionally and personally, that address this very question. Yes, I struggle with the question of, *Am I enough?* And yes, I know that others wrestle with the same question. So what is the answer? How do we begin to address this question? For me, the answer is not about giving a quick yes or no response. It's not about throwing out there a "Yes, I am enough," or "No, I am not enough because I am blind" type of answer. Actually, it is not that simple for any of us. So what is the answer? The answer comes in the form of a shift in mind-set, one that is constantly being lived out throughout our lives. The shift comes as we start to change from a thought pattern of *I am less than and not worthy* to a pattern of *I am equal and I am a worthy human being.* Our thoughts change from *I have nothing to give* to *I am a valuable person who has gifts and talents to share with the world.* We each begin to change from viewing ourselves negatively to viewing ourselves through the truth of who we are.

But the question returned to this: *Am I enough?* I had two

options. I could live believing that I was not enough because I am blind. Or, I could choose each day to know that I am enough because I am a beloved creation of God, one equally worthy with anyone else. I could choose to believe that I am enough because I have gifts and strengths both because of my personality and because of my life experiences. Am I enough? Yes! Are we each enough? Absolutely! Living into the promise that we are enough is a process that must be worked out daily.

Being part of the unit rounds during my chaplain residency helped teach me that indeed I am enough. I learned this while interacting with patients. I quickly learned that what I considered to stop me from being enough was in fact what made me enough. One day, I was called to the pediatric unit. One of the nurses at the central floor station explained that I needed to go see a twelve-year-old patient named Heather. The nurse told me that Heather had an eating disorder. She was not responding to her parents, counselor, social worker, or the nurses. So they wanted the chaplain to visit. When I walked into the room I said, "Heather, I am Reverend Bratton. I am the chaplain for the unit. Could I sit down and chat with you for a few minutes?" She blurted out, "Wait, wait. You are blind?" I immediately thought, *Oh, here we go. She is viewing me as less than because I am blind. This is so frustrating!* Then she said, "You are not going to focus on how I look physically?" I said, "No," still thinking in my head that this was not going to go well. Then Heather said, "Please, stay. I want to talk to you." She turned to her parents, sister, and the nurse and said, "You all can leave." They laughed, and I thought, *OK, maybe she was not thinking less of me.* I sat down in the chair next to Heather and we had a great conversation. Heather was able to open up and share about her eating disorder. We were also able to talk about her relationship with God. Was Heather miraculously healed in that moment? She was not. However,

Heather was willing to open up so the healing process could begin. Now, why did Heather let me in the room? She let me in because of the one part of me that I thought made me "less than." Heather showed me that, indeed, my blindness did not make me "less than." Rather, *I am enough*, even with the fact that I have a disability.

What a powerful lesson Heather taught me and continues to teach me. We all have parts of our lives that we view as "less than" or not worthy. Those parts of our lives that we allow to make us think we are not enough. Heather shows each of us that indeed we are enough. We all face choices. We can choose to complain about those areas of our lives that we perceive make us "less than." Or, we can choose to acknowledge those specific areas and know that we are a whole person, one worthy of respect. I realize this is not an easy choice. In fact, the choice is an incredibly difficult one! It is often easier for us to make the choice to remain in the mind-set of: *Oh, I am not equal to anyone else. I am "less than." I am just going to feel sorry for myself.* But showing moment-by-moment courage is necessary in making the hard but freeing decisions. What freedom and healing comes when we choose to show tenacity, when we determine that, day by day, we are whole individuals worthy of dignity and respect. Rather than exhausting ourselves and putting ourselves down by thinking that we are not enough, we can choose to display the grit that integrates all parts of our lives together.

Similar to my visit with Heather, I had another patient interaction that allowed me to use the one part of myself that I thought prevented me from being enough. Toward the end of my residency the nurses on the orthopedic unit called me and asked me to immediately come to their unit. Once I arrived at the station, several nurses started telling me about Richard. One said, "Please go visit Richard. He is angry with the care he is receiving. He will not follow any of our orders. He keeps saying that we do not understand what he is going through." Once she finished, I asked, "Has he requested a visit from the chaplain?" The nurse quickly said, "Oh no. But we all know you are the only one who might get through to him." Surprised, I said, "Oh, really?" The nurse said, "Well, he is blind, so we hope you are able to help him understand that we are here to help him get better." I thought, *Oh, this is going to either go amazingly well or extremely bad!* So I left the nurses station and went to Richard's room. As I entered I said, "Richard, I am Reverend Bratton, the chaplain on the unit. Can I spend a few moments with you?" Without hesitating, he shouted out, "No! No one understands what I am going through. I am blind and no one knows how to help me." As soon as Richard stopped shouting, I calmly said, "I am blind too." Then I put Jira's leash up on the bed and said, "Here is the leash of my guide dog. Now can I stay and talk for a few minutes?" Completely shocked and taken off guard, Richard said, "You are? Yes, please stay." Then for the next few minutes I listened to Richard as he talked about his anger and frustration. Then I talked about the fact that the nurses and staff were there to help him. Richard had the choice of being angry and refusing their care, or he could choose to feel his anger, let the anger go, and receive the help he needed. Richard was discharged a few days after our conversation, so I did not visit him again. But that one conversation taught me two powerful lessons.

First, I again learned that what I thought made me "less than" could be used as a strength. If I was fully sighted, the nurses would not have called me to go visit Richard. Likewise, Richard would have told me to leave rather than asking me to stay. All of our gifts, talents, and life experiences are constantly woven together to create our unique lives. Does this mean

IT DOES MEAN THAT WE CAN STRIVE TO TAKE THAT ADVERSITY AND TRAUMA AND USE IT TO BETTER OUR LIVES AS WELL AS THE LIVES OF OTHERS.

that we are glad for the adversity and trauma in our lives? Does it mean that we enjoy the challenges in our lives? Of course not. It does mean that we can strive to take that adversity and trauma and use it to better our lives as well as the lives of others.

There was a second lesson from Richard. As I sat in Richard's room, he told me how angry he was that the nurses and staff did not know how to help him because of his blindness. He blamed them for not knowing how to interact with someone who was blind. He yelled at them and then refused to follow their orders because he was mad. He was exhausting himself with anger and frustration. In doing so, Richard was also preventing himself from receiving the health care he needed to get better. I said to him, "So you have told the nurses and staff the best ways to help you? You have shared with them what you need help with and what you do not need help with?" Richard quickly answered: "Of course not! They should just know." I took a breath. "So let me make sure that I understand what is going on," I said. "You are angry, frustrated, and refusing to receive their care because the hospital does not know how best to work with you as a person who is blind. However, you have never communicated your needs?" With frustration in his voice, Richard said, "Right." Having this conversation with Richard was, for me, one of those moments when we give others great advice—then, quickly, we realize that we too need to apply our own advice!

Through my conversation with Richard I learned the value of clearly communicating my needs. Going through the trauma of becoming blind and adapting to life without sight, I now had different needs. As I told Richard, *I* had two choices. I could exhaust myself being angry and frustrated that others did not know how to help me or interact with me. Or I could choose to clearly communicate my needs. During graduate school I learned a technique called non-violent communication (NVC). NVC is centered around the theory of stating our needs with compassion rather than judgment or blame. Of course, I learned NVC so I could help people like Richard communicate their needs rather than exploding at people with anger and frustration. NVC is a powerful tool for me professionally, and it is also a great tool for me personally. Learning how to interact with the world as a professional who is blind was daunting, often overwhelming. Often it seemed easier to default to the mind-set of blaming others for treating me differently and then judging them for viewing me as "less than." In truth, the blaming and judging were not in fact easier—they were *more* exhausting and *less* empowering.

Like most aspects of our lives, there was not one magical moment when I transitioned from always being frustrated about how others viewed me to constantly and clearly communicating my needs. Instead, there are some situations when I get overwhelmed with anger and other times when I calmly state what I need. A perfect example of being filled with anger and judgment was the time I was eating breakfast with a group at a conference for chaplains. We had gathered for breakfast before the day-long conference began. Some of the people I knew well and some I did not know at all. Jennifer, who I had never met, sat down on my right. As soon as she sat down, she looked at me and said in a loud, demanding voice, so that the whole table could hear: "Now, Laura, I want to get the whole story straight. Tell me every detail. How old were you when you became blind? What can you see now? Can you see me? When did you get your guide dog? How does she help you?

How did you get through college and graduate school? I just do not know how you do your job. I mean, how can you do it?" By this point, those at the table had stopped talking and everyone was staring at me. I know my face was bright red and I wanted to crawl under the table and disappear as quickly as possible. Shocked and not knowing what to do, I started answering her questions. With each answer I gave I got more and more angry. *What in the world was she thinking? I mean, really?* Did she not have a clue how strange it is to meet someone and then start bombarding them with questions?

> BY THIS POINT, THOSE AT THE TABLE HAD STOPPED TALKING AND EVERYONE WAS STARING AT ME. I KNOW MY FACE WAS BRIGHT RED AND I WANTED TO CRAWL UNDER THE TABLE AND DISAPPEAR AS QUICKLY AS POSSIBLE.

For the rest of the breakfast and throughout that day I was fuming. I called my close friends and went on and on about this strange and humiliating interaction I had at breakfast. As I reflect on the conversation, I realize I could have handled it better. Rather than answering all of her questions and getting so worked up, I could have clearly stated my feelings and need. Rather than feeling like I was forced to submit to answering all her questions, I could have said, "Jennifer, I appreciate that you are interested in knowing more about how I became blind. I am more than willing to answer all of your questions after breakfast or another time." Then I could have continued the conversation everyone was having at the table. Stating my needs would have taken away all of my anger that continued to explode in my mind the rest of that day!

Often, when we go through adversity and struggles, we get into the mind-set of blaming and judging. We blame others for not knowing how to interact or meet our needs. We judge others for the ways they treat us or interact with us. We get angry, frustrated, and aggravated because of the comments we receive. While it may be true that others make us angry and frustrated with their comments, it is also true that it is our job as individuals to clearly communicate our needs. There is no way that people can know our needs. It is not another person's responsibility to know how to interact with someone with a disability or anyone who is labeled as "different." Rather, it is our responsibility to know our needs and clearly state those needs. Think back to Richard. It was not the responsibility of the nurses and staff at the hospital to know best how to interact with someone who is blind. Instead, it was Richard's responsibility to clearly communicate with the nurses in what ways he needed and did not need help. The same is true for each of us. We have choices each day. We can choose to live a life that blames and judges, or we can choose to live a life that courageously communicates our needs.

WE HAVE CHOICES EACH DAY. WE CAN CHOOSE TO LIVE A LIFE THAT BLAMES AND JUDGES, OR WE CAN CHOOSE TO LIVE A LIFE THAT COURAGEOUSLY COMMUNICATES OUR NEEDS.

There were countless interactions at the hospital, such as those with Heather and Richard, that taught me about being a chaplain, as well as teaching me valuable life lessons. One visit perfectly sums up all of my experiences there. It was early April and I went to visit a patient, Nancy. Nancy was recovering from surgery. Through our entire conversation, Nancy talked about how anxious and nervous she was feeling. She was still anxious from the anticipation of the surgery. She continued to be nervous as she hoped to have a full recovery. After listening to Nancy and discussing different ways she could work through her anxiety, she took a big, deep breath. She said, "Chaplain, I am now completely peaceful. I have not had this much peace in a long time." So what did my mind turn to? I immediately started thinking, *Oh look at me! This Princeton Theological Seminary degree and Cleveland Clinic experience has made me really good. I mean, I am totally getting awesome at this whole chaplain thing.* As I was thinking how great I was, Nancy said, "Your dog has just done everything for me. She is laying there so peacefully on the floor, and she has taken away my anxiety." My first thought was, *Well, good thing I am attached to the leash!* Did Nancy totally burst my bubble or what? There I was thinking about what a great chaplain I was because Nancy was no longer anxious. But the truth was that she was feeling peaceful because of my guide dog quietly lying there on the floor. For the rest of the day, and even now, I laugh at that visit and at myself. How easy it is for us to get so wrapped up in who we think we are and how we think it is all about us. What a great gift Nancy gave me. I am most grateful for the reminder that life is not all about us. Life is not centered around *our* individual lives. Instead, life is about the connection between all of creation.

Going through adversity and trauma can cause us to think that the whole world revolves around our needs. What courage

WHAT A GIFT WHEN WE CAN ZOOM OUT FROM THINKING THAT THE WORLD IS ALL ABOUT US AND KNOW THAT WE ARE EACH A SIGNIFICANT PERSON WHO IS PART OF THE WHOLE OF LIFE.

and strength it takes to be able to laugh at ourselves and not take ourselves so seriously. What a gift when we can zoom out from thinking that the world is all about us and know that we are each a significant person who is part of the whole of life.

Chapter 9

Being Competent

After I completed the chaplain residency at the Cleveland Clinic, I left the world of school and residencies and started my first full-time job. I had been named senior pastor of a United Methodist Church in Greenville, South Carolina. Just a few weeks before starting at the church, I was ordained as a clergy in the United Methodist Church. The ordination process in the UMC is incredibly long and difficult. At minimum, it takes six years to complete while constantly going through interviews, background checks, credit checks, psychological exams, writing papers, and, of course, successfully completing graduate school. So, to make it through the process of ordination was indeed a celebration and honor. I celebrated that I had made it through all the requirements. Most of all, I celebrated and was grateful for my family, friends, home church, and the community that surrounded me during the time I was in the ordination process. There was not one particular situation I was most thankful for; rather, I was grateful for the endless support that enabled me to live out my strengths and gifts.

While I was thankful and celebrated the accomplishment, I was also humbled and honored. What an incredible honor to be charged with the gift of officiating weddings, funerals, weekly worship services, and the sacraments of holy communion and holy baptism. In addition, I was honored to fulfill the responsibility of preaching, teaching, offering pastoral care, and leading the administrative duties of the organization. During the ordination service I was excited, thankful, and honored. But there was also another emotion running through my mind.

> WHILE I WAS THANKFUL AND CELEBRATED THE ACCOMPLISHMENT, I WAS ALSO HUMBLED AND HONORED.

Remember that our journey can be like climbing up a long and treacherous mountain? After a short distance on our way up, we stop and seriously consider running as fast as we can down the mountain rather than using the effort needed to make it to the top. We know that we need to, and want to, get to the summit, but it just seems easier, as though it will require less effort, to run back down to the mountain base and hide. Sitting at the bottom is not where we want to be, but it just seems more comfortable.

Well, standing there on the mountain thinking about whether I should continue hiking up or quickly sprint my way back down—this was my mind-set as I started as pastor of a church. I was anxious and nervous as I thought about the situation. I was the first female pastor in the history of the church. I was also the first young adult pastor in about thirty years, and I was the first pastor with a disability. I was also anxious about starting in my new role as I thought about questions such as: Can I do this? Will I do a good job? Will I be the pastor the members of this church need? I also had other racing questions, such as: Will they receive me as their pastor? Will they treat me different because of my disability? I was as anxious as anyone would be when starting a new profession, and I was especially nervous about how I would be received since I was blind.

The first Sunday arrived and I was a combination of excited, confident, and nervous. I had already spent time at the church getting oriented to the building and the chancel area where I would be preaching and leading worship. I wanted to make sure that my guide dog and I were completely comfortable navigating the surroundings. I also spent what seemed like countless hours working on the sermon. While it was not my first sermon, it was my first sermon as the pastor of a church. Once the sermon was written and rehearsed multiple times, the order of worship for the service completed, and the walk-through of the church building completed, I was ready. Sunday morning arrived and I was in my robe sitting in the chancel area chair in the sanctuary. The pianist was playing music as the worship service started. There was no turning back now! All those thoughts of turning around and running down the mountain were over.

The congregation was filled with church members, many members from my home church, friends who had come to support me on this first Sunday, and the Greenville District superintendent. The district superintendent is the person over all the United Methodist churches in one specific area. Quick translation: He was my boss! Yes, it was my first Sunday ever as pastor of a church, and who is sitting in the congregation? My boss! I thought to myself, *Fabulous! I will be the first in the history of the world to be pastor of a church for a total of one day! Game over.* Or was it? Of course, with my boss sitting in the congregation, my mind started racing to thoughts of judging myself. Thankfully, those thoughts were not actually correct! The district superintendent was not there to judge me; instead, he was there to offer his support. His presence was telling me he supported me as I started this new chapter.

So, once the gathering music stopped, one of the church lay leaders started the announcements and then moved through the other parts of the service. Then came time for the sermon. Right before the sermon and during the time that I was preaching, I was both confident and nervous. I was confident because I had spoken countless times in front of all different sizes of groups. I was nervous because it was my first Sunday as the leader of a church.

> I WAS CONFIDENT BECAUSE I HAD SPOKEN COUNTLESS TIMES IN FRONT OF ALL DIFFERENT SIZES OF GROUPS. I WAS NERVOUS BECAUSE IT WAS MY FIRST SUNDAY AS THE LEADER OF A CHURCH.

Well, I got through that sermon. Was it my best ever? It was not. Did I have perfect diction with appropriate pauses? Absolutely not! Did I make it through? Yes! After a prayer and the congregational closing hymn, the first service was, thankfully, over. I greeted everyone afterward. Most of the church members I was meeting for the first time, and I also was able to speak with those members of my home church and friends who came to offer me support.

The first worship service and the welcome reception went well. The following few weeks also went by without major problems.

So how did my anxiety and fear not become reality? The main reason can be summed up in one word. People! I was nervous that the congregation members would not receive me as their pastor because of two things: I was a young female, and I had a disability. Oh, was I wrong! The leadership of the church as well as the members immediately began treating me as their pastor. They were not focusing on my perceived differences; instead, they focused on how I performed as their spiritual leader. They cared more about the content of my sermons, how I led Bible study, my interactions with the children, and the care I offered the homebound members.

In the church profile that I first read about the church, the congregation wrote about what a loving church they are to all people. I thought to myself, *Well, this is going to be a good test! Will they welcome their own pastor?* Indeed, they put their words into actions and welcomed me warmly. How grateful I am for those who treated me as a whole person. Rather than getting distracted that I was female, young, and disabled, they chose to view me as their leader.

We're often guilty of focusing only on those things that label us as "other" in life. We develop a steady thought pattern that plays over and over in our minds. This pattern focuses on all of the aspects that we believe are working against us. We assume we are going to have a negative experience. What a gift it is when those positive situations and people in our lives break into our thought patterns and show us that we indeed can embrace all of who we are, even those things that we are having serious doubts about. What deep gratitude comes when we experience and know that our whole being is valued. Being grateful for those situations and people who value our lives gives us great courage and endurance—we can continue hiking up the long and sometimes exhausting mountain of life.

There was another key factor that contributed to my positive experience. It too is summed up in a single word: grit! Over the years of going through the experience of becoming blind and adapting to life without sight, I learned how to display the grit needed to be comfortable in my own skin, as well as to clearly state my needs. This means that I choose, every day, to show the courage and determination to be confident in who I am. Yes, being confident even in the fact that I am a person who is blind. Being comfortable in my own skin means that I am confident in my whole being. This takes grit! *Easy* and *quick* are not the words that come to mind when describing how to become comfortable with our lives. Instead, the process is difficult and slow. Yet this process is also healing and empowering. Receiving help physically, emotionally, and spiritually as I adapted to my new normal gave me the grit I needed. I was able to enter my professional role as pastor confident in who I was. I did not start this position by telling people, "Now, I am not really sure if I can do this because I am blind. You all need to be really gentle with me because I am blind." I didn't sit down with the leaders of the church and say, "I want you to know that I am not sure that I can perform because I am blind. So you each will need to do my work for me." Instead, I chose to fully acknowledge my blindness and let the leadership know that, together, we could make the necessary accommodations that I needed.

I had to display another form of grit as well: how to clearly state my needs. Remember Richard, who blamed the nurses for not knowing how to help him? The truth was that he had not expressed his needs. As a person with a disability, I quickly learned that it is my responsibility to know my needs and then clearly communicate those needs to others. So, when starting my position with the church, I did not go to the leadership expecting them to know how best to make accommodations. Instead, it was my responsibility to communicate with them how best they could make accommodations. For example, I asked if the lay leader who was going to be reading the announcements each week could also read the Scripture.

The church was used to the pastor reading the Scripture before the sermon was preached. I explained to them it would be best for me if I could put all my effort into the sermon rather than dividing my effort between the Scripture and the sermon. Thankfully, they had no issues, and we easily made the change. I also let them know that I did not yet *know* all the accommodations I would need! As I discovered areas in which I needed help, I would ask. Thankfully, dealing with needed accommodations was never an issue in my role as pastor with this church.

Clearly stating your needs takes incredible courage and determination because you first must *know* your needs. I had to know that it was best for me to put all of my energy into preparing and preaching the sermon. Could I read the Scripture as well? Absolutely! I could braille it out or have a braille copy of the Bible and read the passage each week. Yes, it was possible, and yet I also had to know that I did not have to spend energy on the passage when I could use that energy in different ways.

So, I learned three valuable lessons from my first job as pastor, as can all of us. First, we learn the value of approaching life, especially new beginnings and unfamiliar circumstances, with a positive perspective. Instead of thinking about a new situation with negative thoughts or doubts, what if we approached the new situation with positive thoughts? For example, I fell into the thought pattern of focusing on what I assumed was going to go wrong. My mind started racing to the negative rather than waiting to allow the situation to unfold. I spent unnecessary energy worrying about things that, in fact, never happened. How much energy can we save when we choose to let go of our preconceptions and live in the present? Does thinking positively about a new situation or circumstance mean the situation will go well just because we have positive thoughts? Absolutely not! It means we spend our energy in different ways. Then, if a negative situation does arise, we have the strength to address the issue in a healthy manner. But warning: choosing to approach new situations with positive thoughts does not come naturally. It requires making an intentional decision to live, daily, with a positive mind-set.

The second lesson we can learn is the value of being grateful for those people who view us as whole people deserving of respect. We are often so busy, and focused on ourselves, or our situations, that we miss the gift of being thankful for those people in our lives who value us for the whole people that we are rather than getting stuck on our differences. The church members gave me the gift of viewing me as a whole

THEY VIEWED ME AS A WHOLE PERSON AS THEY CLEARLY ACKNOWLEDGED MY DISABILITY AND WERE MORE THAN WILLING TO MAKE ANY ACCOMMODATIONS NECESSARY. THEY VIEWED ME AS THEIR PASTOR AS THEY FULLY EXPECTED ME TO USE MY STRENGTHS AND GIFTS AS THEIR LEADER.

person who was now their pastor. They viewed me as a whole person as they clearly acknowledged my disability and were more than willing to make any accommodations necessary. They viewed me as their pastor as they fully expected me to use my strengths and gifts as their leader. They did not minimize any parts of my life or situation. Rather, they embraced all of who I am. So, I had a choice. In fact, we all have a choice. We can choose to move so fast through life that we do not express our deep gratitude for those people who embrace our lives. Or, we can choose to acknowledge those people in our lives who do, in fact, value all that we are—and tell them that we are thankful. What strength we receive when we choose to take the time to be grateful for the respect that we receive from other people. How do we express our appreciation? Does our whole world have to stop while we display some huge, grand expression of gratitude? It's not that complicated. Instead, our gratefulness can be woven throughout the moments of our daily lives.

We can express appreciation in countless ways. We can journal about all the people and aspects of our lives that bring us gratitude. We can pray prayers of thanksgiving or spend time in meditation expressing our thanks. We can also express our appreciation when we are with the person, or we can write a letter, note, call, email, text, or use any other form of communication. The particular method that we use to express our gratitude is not the main focus. Rather, the important thing is that we each choose to take the time to express our thankfulness for the people in our lives who value us. Will we always perfectly choose to express our gratitude? Of course not. Should we strive to make the choice of showing thanks in our daily lives? Of course.

As we each choose to take the time to express our gratefulness, we receive courage and strength. Facing new situations in life or going through adversity and trauma can make us feel isolated or lonely. It's easy to slip into the mind-set of thinking that no one understands. We think, *I am all alone as I deal with this particular situation in my life.* So, how can gratitude help us in those times? Being grateful and taking the time to express our gratitude creates the opportunity to remember that we are not isolated or alone. Yes, our specific situation and circumstances are unique to our lives. Yes, it is true that we are the only ones who can fully know what we are going through. But no, we are not isolated and alone. Through

177

the gift of gratefulness we become aware of those people and situations that remind us that we are indeed whole human beings. Through the power of gratitude we are able to shift from a viewpoint that magnifies our isolation and loneliness to a viewpoint that zooms out and shows us that our lives are deeply interwoven with other people and with all creation.

The third lesson is to learn how to show grit as we accept ourselves. Just as we have the choice to express our gratitude, we each have the choice to display the grit of self-acceptance. We can choose to go through life fighting against our lives and not embracing all of who we are. Or, we can choose to show grit, which gives us the ability to accept ourselves. We all have interacted with people who choose to fight against themselves or others or simply show no confidence in who they are. When we view such people, we see that they are typically negative and angry. Regardless of the situation, they find something to be negative about or angry over. Then there are those people we interact with who have zero confidence in themselves. Their shoulders are slouched, their head is down, and their overall appearance shows that they do not have self-confidence. They are often down on themselves and belittle their strengths and gifts. And we also know those people who embrace all of the different aspects of their lives. They have a positive outlook, clearly know their strengths and weaknesses, laugh at themselves, and are energizing to be around. So which choice are we going to make? How are we going to go through life?

Choosing to have grit,

WE HAVE THE FREEDOM TO CHANGE AND GROW IN WHO WE ARE. RATHER THAN BEING RESTRICTED BY ANGER, NEGATIVITY, SELF-DOUBT, OR ANYTHING ELSE, WE ARE FREE TO GROW AND CHANGE.

which gives us the ability to accept ourselves, is not a one-time, easy, or quick decision. It's just the opposite! Accepting ourselves is a daily choice that we live out during the course of our lives. The decision takes courage, strength, and endurance. Choosing to have the grit of self-acceptance gives us incredible freedom. We are free to embrace all of who we are. Yes, we can accept those areas that we love about our lives, and yes, we can accept those places and areas of our lives that we do not love. We have the freedom to change and grow in who we are. Rather than being restricted by anger, negativity, self-doubt, or anything else, we are free to grow and change.

RIGHT BEFORE I WALKED INTO THE ROOM TO BEGIN, ONE OF THE MEN WHO WORKED AT THE FACILITY SAID, "YOU JUST SEEM OK WITH BEING BLIND. YOU JUST SEEM TO BE PEACEFUL WITH IT ALL."

Choosing daily to display the grit of self-acceptance gives us the courage to be confident in those areas of our lives that others might label as different. For example, I was able to start my job as a pastor comfortable with who I was because I had chosen daily to have courage, strength, and perseverance. Also, I had chosen to believe the promise that I am a beloved child of God regardless of my disability. I was also able to be comfortable in my own skin because of the support of others. I still laugh when I think about a comment I once received. I was speaking to a group of about a hundred people. Right before I walked into the room to begin, one of the men who worked at the facility said, "You just seem OK with it." I must have looked shocked and confused, because he then said, "You just seem OK with being blind. You just seem to be peaceful with it all." I smiled, nodded my head, and said, "Yes." Then I continued into the room. Indeed, I *am*

OK with being blind. And yes, I am peaceful with it all. Does this mean I like being blind and would choose it? Absolutely not! Are there times when I am not OK with being blind and am anything but peaceful? Of course! But I remain comfortable in who I am, and doing so means that we are confident in our ability to have courage, strength, tenacity, and endurance regardless of the situations we face.

Does having the grit of self-acceptance mean all will go well in our lives? It does not. Having the grit of self-acceptance means, in fact, that we have what it takes to work through adversity, trauma, and anything we will face in life. Having courage and endurance means that the struggles in life will not permanently affect our self-confidence. Rather, we will have the strength to continue moving forward, striving to live with meaning and purpose.

Oh, how my initial anxieties about how I would be received as pastor were completely wrong! Rather than the fears coming true, I was given three incredible life lessons that greatly helped my life. What a gift when we can each learn to have a positive mind-set when facing new situations, learn to express deep gratitude for those people in our lives who value our whole being, and learn to show the grit of self-acceptance.

I think back to the words my disability coordinator at Arizona State told me. She said, "Laura, you have gone through the initial process of grieving your vision. I just want you to know that you will continue to grieve forever. As you come to a new stage in your life you will grieve that you do not have your vision." Also, I think back to the words of wisdom that I received from my supervisor, Dr. Griesel: "Laura, I want you to never forget that one important fact. Over the internship you have proven that you can do the work. From this point forward, no matter what you face or who you encounter, never forget that you can do the work." These powerful words of wisdom ran through my mind during the first year I served as a pastor. They gave me strength and perseverance. I held tightly to my disability coordinator's words because I often found myself in a place of frustration and grief. Once again I was in a new chapter of my life. A new chapter in which I was a church pastor! As I learned all the different parts involved in leading a church, I had to learn how to make the necessary accommodations so I could perform each task. I would get frustrated that I had to go to the extra effort of making accommodations. It was easy to think: *Oh, this is requiring so much extra effort. My other colleagues don't have to spend half as much effort on the same tasks. I could do this so much faster if I could see.* These racing thoughts of frustration indeed moved me to the place my disability coordinator told me that I would be. Yes, I was again in a new chapter of my life, and I was grieving that I did not have my vision. Remembering those words of wisdom gave me the permission to acknowledge those thoughts, feel the grief, and let it go. When we experience adversity and trauma in our lives that forces us into a new reality, we are constantly adjusting to the new normal. Even when the new normal does not seem new anymore, we are continually adjusting and adapting with every new chapter in our lives.

So how do we respond? How do we move forward yet again? We move ahead by remembering those times in which we have already adapted. We access the courage and strength that we have used before to again tackle this new chapter. Accessing the determination and perseverance is like starting a new exercise program. When we first start working out we are completely out of shape. After any form of exercise we are out of breath, exhausted, sore, and totally doubting our decision to start this entire exercise thing! Then after days, weeks, and months go by, we build up strength. We are not as quick to be out of breath, exhausted, or have sore muscles. Yes, we can still feel the workout, but we are building from a stronger and more healthy base. Instead of feeling the pain of the workout, we feel the benefits. We are able to breathe easier, sleep better, have more energy, and feel healthier. Then we might decide to start a completely different form of exercise. We go from running to swimming. We knew how to run, and now it is time to learn a new form of exercise. So, beginning to swim is like starting all over again. We go back to that place of being out of breath and exhausted. We again think: *What in the world am I doing? I knew how to run, but now I am back to square one.* However, there is one major difference. Yes, we are out of breath and exhausted because of the new exercise. But no, we are not completely back to square one. We have the foundation built from all the time we spent running. We now have a much stronger and confident overall base. Yes, we know it is going to hurt and be exhausting. Yes, we know that we will have those times when we doubt our decision to start a new form of exercise. Yet we also know that we have what we need to learn a new exercise regimen. We know we have what it takes and that we will greatly benefit from the results.

Facing a new chapter in our lives is like going from running to swimming. We have chosen to show great courage and endurance as we initially adjusted to a new reality. Then, we find ourselves again at a new chapter in our lives. We are overwhelmed by the present situation and circumstance. We begin to doubt that we can adapt and adjust yet again. We jump back into that negative mind-set. We have racing thoughts, such as: *I cannot do this. The effort is going to be exhausting, so I am not even going to try.* Or, *quitting now would just be easier.*

Then, through the grit given to us by other people, as well as gained in ourselves, our thoughts begin to change. We remember the courage and strength that we previously displayed in our lives. We also remember those people in our lives who loved us enough not to let us quit. The love, support, and encouragement of other people give us the strength to continue forward. Then, moment by moment and day by day, we are able to adapt and adjust to our new normal.

Reflecting on those most difficult and challenging times allows us to remember the tenacity and endurance we hold within ourselves. We know that we can indeed face this new chapter in our lives. We can access the strength of others as well as our own strength. As we face a new chapter, we can draw from the courage we have already experienced. Next, we can know that we are building from a strong base. Just as with starting a new form of exercise, we can know that we are not facing this new chapter from square one. Rather, we are starting from a strong base—one that includes grit and gratitude.

For me, starting in the role as a church leader, I was yet again facing a new chapter. A chapter in which I would have to adapt and adjust. I could choose to be permanently overwhelmed, or I could choose to build from my strong foundation. Through the love, support, courage, and determination of my family, friends, and community, I knew that I had what I needed to adjust to *any* new situation.

Another form of strength I received as I adjusted that first year came through the support of family and friends. Throughout my entire first year many people came to worship, such as friends from the adult Sunday school classes from my home church, and the young adult Sunday school class from my home church, which mostly included people that I grew up with, other childhood friends, and neighbors. One particular Sunday I knew that a Sunday school class from my home church was coming to worship. While I was in my office preparing for worship, I could hear everyone gathering in the sanctuary. As soon as I heard everyone talking, I started laughing as I thought to myself, *Really, Laura? You are serious-*

ly asking yourself if you have the strength to yet again adapt to a new situation? Thirty people from your home church have come to support you. No one forced or even asked them to come. They made that decision on their own. They are here to show you support. You have the support that you need to face a new situation. As I stood there in my office, I had one of those moments that is a total reality check. What strength I received from the support shown by others.

Just as friends came to worship, I had many different family members come throughout that first year. One Sunday is etched in my memory forever. The first Sunday in May my father's side of our family decided they would all come to worship. I am not exaggerating when I say that fifty family members came to worship. I know! It sounds like a ridiculous number, but it is true! They all drove about an hour and a half to come to worship—and that is not even the amazing part. The true miracle was that every last person was on time! Have you ever tried to get your family in one place at one time? It often seems next to impossible! Yet, there they were, fifty of my family members gathered on time for worship! Once worship was over and I greeted everyone, my family gathered at my house for lunch. It just so happened that the same Sunday was Boy Scout Sunday at my home church. They were serving homemade box lunches. So they received quite the order from my family that day! Lunch was a chaotic, fun time of enjoying the delicious lunches, catching up, and playing with my young cousins. You know

> I AM NOT EXAGGERATING WHEN I SAY THAT FIFTY FAMILY MEMBERS CAME TO WORSHIP. I KNOW! IT SOUNDS LIKE A RIDICULOUS NUMBER, BUT IT IS TRUE!

those situations when everything comes together better than you could have imagined? When everything perfectly falls into place? Well, that Sunday with my family was one of those days.

Why did my family make the effort? Why did my eighty-four-year-old great aunt, all the way down to infant-age cousins, come to join me in worship? Why did other family members throughout the year come to worship? Did they come to hear some life-changing sermon or have the most powerful worship experience of their lives? Not exactly! They each made the incredible effort because of their love and support for me. They were each saying through their actions: Laura, we love you and support you no matter what.

> THEY EACH MADE THE INCREDIBLE EFFORT BECAUSE OF THEIR LOVE AND SUPPORT FOR ME. THEY WERE EACH SAYING THROUGH THEIR ACTIONS: LAURA, WE LOVE YOU AND SUPPORT YOU NO MATTER WHAT.

no matter what. Wow! What a gift! Saying that I was thankful does not even come close to expressing my deep gratitude. There are just not adequate words to say thank you for these situations.

My first year being a pastor was challenging and exhausting as I adjusted to my new professional role. There were also incredible moments of strength and courage as well as moments of gratitude. For all of us, adapting to a new chapter in our life is indeed like starting a new form of exercise. We will be exhausted and frustrated. We will resist the new chapter because it is hard and uncomfortable. We will want to throw in the towel and quit. Yet . . . we will remember the strength and courage that we displayed in previous situations. Then we will start entertaining the thought that, just maybe, we do have what it takes to adapt. The love, support, and encouragement of others, combined with our own determination, endurance, and gratefulness is exactly what we need to face life's new chapters.

Chapter 10

Grieving Deeply

That first year as a pastor was a combination of feeling frustrated, exhausted, empowered, and grateful. The second year, I experienced one of the most difficult times in my life. But it had nothing to do with being a pastor or my role as church leader.

When I was at Guide Dogs for the Blind receiving my guide dog, Jira, there were several people in the class who were getting their second or third dogs. Throughout class they would talk about how difficult it was when their first guide dog was no longer able to work and then died. Separately, they would each say to me, "Laura,

SEPARATELY, THEY WOULD EACH SAY TO ME, "LAURA, WHEN JIRA DIES IT WILL BE LIKE BECOMING BLIND AGAIN. YOU WILL GRIEVE JUST LIKE YOU DID WHEN YOU ADJUSTED TO LIFE WITHOUT SIGHT."

when Jira dies it will be like becoming blind again. You will grieve just like you did when you adjusted to life without sight. Laura, a part of you will die." Then as I left guide dog school and started college at Arizona State University, other guide dog users that I met would say the same thing. Throughout the next ten years, other guide dog users would talk about the hard, grieving process that they experienced. My close friend, Rebecca, also went through the horrible time of the death of her guide dog. She told me, "Laura, I am here to support you when you have to go through this process." As people shared their pain and sadness with me, I would think to myself, *I hear what you are saying. It is going to be hard.* I also thought, *I have been through countless counseling sessions to learn how to work through the grieving process, so I have learned the techniques that I need. I have a great family and friend support system. I am grounded in my faith. People, I will be just fine!* I could not have been more wrong. Not only were they right, they were barely touching the surface of the deep impact that the death of Jira would have on my life.

On my birthday I was taking the day off from work. Jira was just not acting like herself. For the past few days, I noticed she had been panting much more than normal, and I felt a lump on the side of her neck. She had several fatty tumors before, so I was not too concerned. But it was obvious she was now uncomfortable and panting even more.So I called the veterinarian's office and got an appointment for that afternoon. After closely examining Jira, Dr.

Marshall gave me a prescription and said, "Laura, give this to Jira for the next two days. Then let's see if there are any results." After the vet appointment, I called Jira's craniosacral therapist and told her the situation. So we set up an appointment for Friday afternoon. Tammy had treated Jira multiple times, so I knew a treatment would give us answers. Needless to say, I was not exactly in a cheerful mood when my family gathered for my birthday dinner that night. I was nervous and worried. However, I was not even thinking that Jira was truly seriously ill. I am sure this feeling was both a combination of denial and optimism.

Friday morning, my brother called and asked if I wanted to go to lunch with him, my sister-in-law, and two nieces. Lunch was fun and perfectly normal. Jira guided me well. We all got out of the car at the sandwich shop and my two-year-old niece wanted me to carry her. So, I carried her through the parking lot and into the restaurant while Jira guided me perfectly. I thought to myself: *Oh, there is nothing wrong with Jira. If she had something wrong she would not be guiding me this well.* After lunch, I went straight to Jira's craniosacral appointment. After treating Jira for a few minutes, Tammy said, "Laura, let me tell you what I am feeling." I knew by the tone of her voice that it was not good. She said, "The lump on her neck does seem to be cancer that has spread to her lungs." Right there, I began sobbing. I could not find the strength for another breath. I knew it right then. There was no denying it. Reality hit . . . hard. Jira was extremely ill. Her working life was over. Tammy then said, "Call the vet office and see when you can go back for an appointment."[10] Through the sob-

WORDS JUST CANNOT DESCRIBE WHAT I FELT IN THAT MOMENT. I WAS FROZEN. I WAS IN SHOCK. I COULD NOT THINK OR PROCESS.

bing, I called the vet's office. I got an appointment for one hour later. Words just cannot describe what I felt in that moment. I was frozen. I was in shock. I could not think or process. An hour later I was sitting in one of the examining rooms in the vet office. Dr. Marshall walked into the room with the X-ray results. She said, "Laura, the results show what Tammy found. Jira does have a malignant tumor on her neck and the cancer has spread to her lungs." Then Dr. Marshall said the news that I was not prepared to receive. "Jira has two weeks to live. We are going to keep her as comfortable as possible. While she will not be able to work full-time, you can work her a small amount as she wants to work." My whole world stopped. I sat there in the chair of the vet's office holding Jira's leash, physically shaking, emotionally frozen. Dr. Marshall then wrote out all the instructions for Jira's pain medicine, because I knew I could not remember anything. My whole world had just changed.

Once the appointment was over, I told my immediate family the news. I was in too much shock to do anything but state the facts. I could not cry, scream, bargain, or show any emotion. As soon as I was home, who was the first person I called? My close friend, Rebecca, who had said she would support me through the process. I called her and, thankfully, Rebecca answered. I said, "Well, this is the phone call I never wanted to make." Then I started sobbing. She knew what I meant. She did not know the exact details of the past few days. But Rebecca knew what I was going through. She calmly reassured me that she was there to support me through this horrible time. Rebecca said, "I want you to call the guide dog school and tell them the news. Then call me back." I was both too upset and shocked to ask questions or challenge anything she was saying. So I ended the call and made another most difficult call. The school asked for the veterinarian's office to send a copy of Jira's X-ray results. They told me they would be in touch once they received the records.

Surprisingly, over the next week, Jira acted much better. She stopped panting and seemed to feel much better. Obviously, I did not work her full-time, but I did work her several times. She did great! There was not any change in her work. As each day went by, I thought, *Oh, we have so much longer than two weeks.* I even called the vet to let them know how much better she was doing. I thought, *We totally have a few months. I mean, she is acting like herself and her work is fine.* Then my mind went all the way to the thought there was no way she only had a week to live. I was sure she had lots of time.

But after ten days the panting came back, and I could tell she was extremely uncomfortable. She could not lie still. She would lie down, get up, lie down, get up, repeating this often. On a Tuesday night, I was up with her all night. She did not lie down for more than five minutes at a time. After a few hours I called my parents and asked one of them to come over and spend the night. I was hoping they could see something I was missing that would help Jira. I knew it was a false hope, but I was desperate to do anything to make her more comfortable. Unfortunately, there was nothing I was missing. She continued to be incredibly uncomfortable.

Then, Wednesday morning, she ate some of her food, but not as much as normal. By 10 in the morning she made a huge transition from getting up and down repeatedly to barely being able to get up on her own. Of course, I called the vet, and Dr. Marshall gave me instructions on increasing the pain medication. She added, "Call me at 4:30 this afternoon and let's see how Jira is doing." By 1 that afternoon she could not get up at all by herself. As she was laying there on the floor, I walked up with her favorite treat. A carrot! As I bent down and put this treat in front of her face, with her mouth completely closed, she turned her head away. At that moment I knew what Jira was telling me. She was letting me know she was ready to die. I stood up with the carrot in my hand and said to my dad, "Call mom to come over. It is not going to be long." So my mom immediately left her work and rushed to my house. I spent the afternoon holding Jira. I

I SPENT THE AFTERNOON HOLDING JIRA. I COULD NOT LEAVE HER SIDE. SHE HAD LITERALLY BEEN ON MY LEFT SIDE FOR THE PAST TEN YEARS, SO I WAS GOING TO BE BY HER SIDE DURING THESE LAST HOURS.

could not leave her side. She had literally been on my left side for the past ten years, so I was going to be by her side during these last hours.

At 4:30 that afternoon I called Dr. Marshall to let her know how much Jira had declined. Dr. Marshall, full of compassion, said, "Laura, we are now at that point where we have to make a decision." After a few minutes of talking with the veterinarian, I decided to bring Jira in the following morning at 7 so Dr. Marshall could administer the medicine that would end Jira's suffering and give her a peaceful death.

Around 8 that night, I got Jira's favorite blanket and put it under her so she could sleep on it for her last night. I lay down on the floor beside Jira. I did not sleep one second that night. I held Jira, saying, "It is OK for you to die. You can let go, girl. You have perfectly guided me for ten years. Thank you, thank you, J-girl, for being my eyes. I will be fine because I know that your spirit will never leave me. I am going to miss you more than anything." I went back and forth all night from talking to her, thanking her, sobbing, and being completely silent. As the night went on I could feel Jira becoming more and more lifeless.

At 6:45 a.m. my dad picked Jira up and my mom and I walked behind them to the car. During the ten minutes it took to get to the veterinarian's office, I was numb and completely focused on Jira. All of my energy was focused on her, keeping her comfortable. A few minutes later I was standing in an examining room in the veterinarian office with Jira lifelessly lying on the table in front of me. I continued to pet her, thank her, and tell her how much I loved her. A few minutes after Dr. Marshall administered the IV, she quietly and compassionately said, "Jira's pulse has stopped." For the first instant I felt relieved that Jira was out of pain. She was no longer suffering. Then the reality hit hard. Jira was dead. I started sobbing and continued to tell Jira how much I loved her. Then came the hardest moment, one I was not prepared for. I had to walk away. I had to walk away with Jira's body lying there on the table. How could I do that? How could I possibly walk away with my eyes lying there? After a few minutes my mom came into the room and said, "Laura, it is time to go." With both of us crying, we turned and walked out of the room and to the car. Again, I was in shock. Yes, my body was walking, but my mind was not processing what I was doing. I spent the rest of the day on the floor of my den, holding Jira's blanket. I would have times I was sobbing so hard I could not take a breath. Then I would have other moments when I just felt numb.

I was suddenly where so many guide dog users told me I would be. I was entering into a place of deep grieving. Jira's death was, in fact, just like adjusting to life yet again without sight. In the following days, weeks, and months I was gripped emotionally by panic attacks, shock, sadness, and fear. I also felt the grief in my body as, physically, I could not eat, and it felt like there was a two-ton weight attached to my body. I could not think clearly. A few weeks after Jira died I was standing in front of the washing machine needing to put the clothes in the washer into the dryer. I could not think what to do. I was frozen mentally and physically. I had to tell myself: Take your hand and open up the washer, reach in, get out the clothes, and then bend over to put them in the dryer. Performing this simple and routine action was suddenly hard and required incredible effort.

We all have times in which life is hard and stressful. Life seems overwhelming. Then we have times of deep loss that penetrate to the core of our being. It is like we are thrown back into the ocean water and we are swimming against the current. Actually, we don't even have the strength to try to swim; it is more like we are in the ocean while the huge waves are crashing over and around us. We are in a time of deep grief and loss. The feelings of anger, sadness, loneliness, anxiety, fear, and hopelessness dominate our mind, body, and spirit. In times of intense grief, what do we do? How do we work through the grief? How can we feel the difficult emotions and then adjust to the new normal? As we work through the grieving process we need the support, love, and presence of family, friends, and community. We also need professional help from people who are trained in grief work. In such an intense time of shock and sadness we need the loving actions of others to hold us. We are not in a normal state of mind to make clear decisions or rational choices.

In those first few days and weeks after Jira died, I was indeed held by the love of my family, friends, and others. My parents faithfully sat with me, cried with me, and made sure I was eating and drinking at least a small amount. My brother, sister-in-law, and nieces were a great support as they would bring dinner over and listen while I talked about Jira. My immediate family was once again the strong and constant foundation I needed. My extended family also supported me in countless ways. We all have those moments in life that are just not planned. Those moments of support and love that come in totally unexpected ways and are just what we need in that moment. Well, I did indeed have moments like that. Friday afternoon, the day after Jira died, I received a phone call from the vet's office. "Laura, Jira's ashes are ready." I was going through the motions and answered, "OK, thank you." I hung up and began sobbing. *Jira's ashes are ready? What do you mean? You mean that Jira is better and I can come pick her up from the vet's office?* Hearing the reality of the words, I collapsed on the couch.

After receiving Jira's ashes, I held tightly to the box the whole way home. Once my parents and I pulled in my driveway, we walked inside without saying a word. Right after the front door was closed, the bell rang. Who was at the door? We were just there less than a minute ago, and no one had been approaching the door. My dad opened it, and I heard someone say, "These are for Laura Bratton." My dad thanked the delivery person and then walked into the den with a big flower arrangement for me. My mom read the card. One of my aunts, uncle, and cousin had sent the flowers. Indeed, it was one of those moments you just cannot plan. My family did not know that I was getting Jira's ashes that day. No one tried to time it so I would receive the flowers when I got the ashes. Well, maybe a person did not. But Jira's spirit, and the spirit of love, did indeed know this perfect timing. The timing of receiving the flowers could not have been better. As I walked in the door with Jira's ashes, I received flowers. I cannot put in words how this moment helped me so much.

Another of those moments happened the following Sunday. Two months earlier, I had scheduled my cousin to come to church and sing in worship. We planned for her to come on September 9. As it was obvious that Jira was getting worse, I contacted Annie and we reworked the worship service so that the service was music and Scripture, because I would not be able to preach. When that Sunday morning came, Annie and her thirteen-year-old son, Brad, came to my house. I was still in such shock that I did not realize the deep time of grief I was just beginning to enter. Once at church we got everything ready for the service and were in my office. Not able to feel any emotion, I said to Annie and Brad, "I just do not know what to do. I am missing something." With Brad sitting across my office on the couch and Annie standing beside me at my desk, she compassionately and confidently said, "Laura, you do not need to do anything. We are here to support you." She was right. I did not need to do anything in that moment except allow their support to carry me. I was also right; I was indeed missing something. Jira was not with me. Rather than Jira standing on my left side and a leash in my left hand, I was holding a white cane in my right hand. I had not used a cane in ten years. Well, let's be honest! I had really never used a cane. Yes, I knew all the techniques of using a cane, but I had never used one, except when my orientation and mobility instructors made me do so! So, yes, standing there in my office, I was missing something. The physical eyes that I

> I WAS INDEED MISSING SOMETHING. JIRA WAS NOT WITH ME. RATHER THAN JIRA STANDING ON MY LEFT SIDE AND A LEASH IN MY LEFT HAND, I WAS HOLDING A WHITE CANE IN MY RIGHT HAND. I HAD NOT USED A CANE IN TEN YEARS.

had depended on through high school were nowhere close to useful. The eyes of Jira that I had depended on for the last ten years were suddenly gone.

The reality of this situation continued to overwhelm me as I led the worship service. At one moment, as I sat down in my chair, I reached down to hook the leash to a chair leg. Only there was no leash to hook. When I stood up to walk to the pulpit I stepped around the place where Jira would lay. As I spoke and prayed, Jira was not a few feet away, snoring. (Yes! She seriously snored as I led worship! Needless to say, Jira always honestly told me what she thought of my preaching and praying!) Then, during the last hymn, I reached down to unhook the leash so I could walk down to the front of the sanctuary and give the benediction and then walk to the back of the church to greet everyone. Again, there was no leash to unhook and no Jira to guide me down the stairs and down the sanctuary aisle. The reality of Jira's death was made real in those moments.

AGAIN, THERE WAS NO LEASH TO UNHOOK AND NO JIRA TO GUIDE ME DOWN THE STAIRS AND DOWN THE SANCTUARY AISLE. THE REALITY OF JIRA'S DEATH WAS MADE REAL IN THOSE MOMENTS.

Just like receiving the flowers, the timing of Annie coming to sing at church was better than we could have planned. The presence of Annie and Brad at worship gave me the strength and courage I needed. Once again, God's powerful spirit of love was surrounding me during such an intense time of grieving.

After experiencing my new reality of Jira's passing, I knew I was nowhere close to being able to work. So I took the week off. Waking up in the morning, getting dressed, and trying to eat some breakfast absolutely exhausted me. All week I went

back and forth from sobbing to having no words to laughing about stories of Jira. I continued to live into the horrible
reality that Jira was gone. Even though she did not guide me
around the house, I was constantly aware of her presence. At
6 in the morning and 4 in the afternoon, I would put food in
Jira's bowl. Yet now there was no Jira to come devour the food.
Every few hours I would think, *Oh no! I have not taken Jira
outside in a while.* Then I remembered there was no Jira to
take outside. I would step on one of her bones and say, "Jira,
girl, come get your bone!" Yet there was no Jira to come get
her bone. Throughout that week, I continued to be held by the
love and strength of my family. My uncle drove two hours that
Sunday to bring food and just sit with me. Tuesday afternoon,
two of my aunts also drove two hours to bring me lunch and
spend time with me. I was held by family and I was also held
by friends. Just as Rebecca promised, she was an incredible
support to me. She called each day. She knew what it was like
to go through this death. She could listen to me and give me
words of strength and comfort.

But of all people, perhaps, Jira's puppy raisers were the most
powerful support for me. They had raised Jira from the time
she was eight weeks old until she was sixteen months. Even
though they were across the country, their support was just
what I needed. We cried as we talked about the ways Jira had
touched and changed our lives. We laughed about the difficult
puppy that Jira was to raise! We talked about our deep sadness
as we thought about living without our "J-girl."

The week away from the normal routine of life gave me
the space to begin a grieving process that would continue for
months to come. Life now did indeed feel like I was thrown
out of the boat into the deep waves of ocean water. The comfort and security of the boat was stripped away and I was sinking in the rough, salty water. As I seemed to be sinking I was

held only by the anchor line of family and friends. During deep times of grieving in our lives, it often feels like we are sinking as ocean waves crash around us. We are not able to sustain our normal mental, emotional, physical, and spiritual strength. And it is in those times that we are dependent on the love and courage of others. The actions of others create the anchor line that prevents us from sinking. We will indeed stay afloat because the strength of the anchor line is stronger than the waves.

In the days, weeks, and months after Jira died, I lived into the reality that other guide dog users said I would experience. I was grieving that part of me that had died. Why was Jira's death so difficult? Why was I again grieving my vision loss while also knowing a part of me had died? I had received Jira just as my vision had been declining significantly. It was not safe for me to navigate my surroundings without a guide dog or cane. Emotionally, it was a time of working through the difficult process of living life with limited sight. I was over-whelmed with anxiety, fear, and depression. I was in the midst of learning how to cope and move forward with life. Then I received Jira, who gave me the gift of independence, freedom, and confidence. Jira showed me that I could once again nav-igate any surroundings independently. I did not have to be dependent on others to help me. As Jira gave me confidence in my physical abilities, she also gave me confidence emotional-ly. I started to gain confidence once again within myself. I was able to more fully accept my new reality. Receiving Jira gave me the courage and strength I needed to move forward. Jira was a huge part of my healing process; she showed me the way forward, literally, both physically and emotionally.

So grieving her death was, once again, like adjusting to life without sight. I was immediately thrown back into the world of needing help to navigate my surroundings. I ei-

ALL OF A SUDDEN I WAS WALKING SLOWER, MUCH MORE CAUTIOUS, AND MUCH MORE FEARFUL. FOR THE FIRST TIME IN MY LIFE I TRULY FELT DISABLED.

ther had to use my cane or do sighted guide. Sighted guide is a technique where the person who is blind holds the elbow of the sighted person. All of a sudden I was walking slower, much more cautious, and much more fearful. For the first time in my life I truly felt disabled. Jira and I had become one unit in the past ten years. I did not realize just how much she helped me to move and navigate in a normal way. Obviously, I initially felt the huge difference of working with a guide dog. Then, as we became a team, I did not realize just how much Jira gave me the ability to live life normally. Whether I was walking to class in 110 degrees in Arizona, walking to class in 20 degrees and a few inches of snow at Princeton, walking through minus-5 degrees with a wind of 30 miles per hour with three feet of snow on the ground in Cleveland . . . walking from my office to the sanctuary at church . . . or just shopping or hiking with friends, Jira was always there, allowing me to navigate anything. If I tripped or was about to fall, I would lean into the harness I was holding and be just fine. So, indeed, I was grieving the ability Jira gave me to live a full life.

As I grieved the physical help that Jira gave me, I also grieved the loss of her presence. She brought me so much joy, laughter, and gave me opportunities to meet people and experience situations I would not have experienced. She gave me so much joy and laughter as we would play with her toys and she would run around like crazy. Somehow, playing with Jira just made those bad test grades in college not so bad! I would think it was the end of the world when I failed a Geology 101 exam. Then, playing with Jira and her toys reminded me that I would actually be just fine!

Through Jira I met people I otherwise would not have met. For example, it was graduation night from guide dog school and I was eating dinner with Jira's puppy raisers. I was talking about starting college soon at Arizona State University. Caroline said, "Oh, Laura, my sister lives in Phoenix. She and her husband have two daughters a few years younger than you." Caroline gave me her contact information and said we needed to meet. I did get to meet Becky and her family. They became close friends of mine and a great support for me while I was in college. Even since college we have stayed connected. Becky and her family also loved meeting me because they got to see Jira! They met Jira several times when she was a puppy since Becky's sister was Jira's puppy raiser. The first time I met Stacey, one of Becky's daughters, she said to me, "So, I am still working to forgive Jira." Thinking it was going to be something horrible, I said, "Oh no, what did she do?" Stacey then said, "Well, when we were at Caroline's house, Jira got one of my favorite flip-flops out of my suitcase and ate it!" Not even thinking about it, in my most southern voice, I looked down to where Jira was lying and said, "Jira Bratton, say you are sorry right now, young lady!" Stacey burst out laughing. I think it was the first time in her life she had heard someone from the deep South reprimand a person or animal. I mean, I only tripled the amount of syllables for each word while using Jira's first and last name. I did not think that was strange! I had only lived out of the South for a few months. Needless to say, my reaction more than made up for the flip-flop that Jira destroyed.

Thankfully, Jira did more for all of us than just chew Stacey's flip-flop. Through meeting Jira as a puppy, Becky and her family decided to also become puppy raisers. A few months after we met, they received their first puppy. We were a support to each other throughout the process. As Becky and her family raised their puppy, Jira was right there to remind them of the important role of puppy raisers. Without puppy raisers I would not have had the gift of Jira. So on those days when their puppy was chewing things up and not listening to their commands, I would remind them of the reason they were going through this process.

Just as Jira served as a reminder of why Becky and her family were going through the effort of raising a puppy, I too learned so much about the puppy raising phase. Obviously, I had just learned about the power of the guide dog and all the training that is required. However, I knew nothing of the time and effort that people put into each dog for the first twelve to fifteen months of the dog's life. I quickly gained an even deeper appreciation for all the people who are involved in the process of raising and training a guide dog. The puppy raisers spend an incredible amount of time and resources so that people like me can receive guide dogs.

* * * * * * *

There is one example that perfectly sums up the gift that Jira and I were to Becky and her family as they raised puppies—and the gift they were to me as a new guide dog handler. Once a group of puppies is ready to go to guide dog school, the school will send a truck to pick up the dogs. That day is called Puppy Truck Day. Obviously, it is an extremely difficult day as the families say good-bye to the dogs they have loved and taken care of for the past many months. Even though they knew when they were getting the dog that the dog would not be with them forever, it is still an incredibly difficult day.

I had the gift of being part of several Puppy Truck Days. I

would be there for no other reason than to remind each family why they were doing what they were doing. I could not be standing there at Puppy Truck Day with my guide dog without the previous time and effort that each person had put into the puppies! Did it make the tears and sadness go away? No. But the purpose is for each person to be reminded of the gift they are giving to another person. As I was there at Puppy Truck Day, I received the gift of giving out the new puppies to the families. The guide dog school representatives would hand me the puppy, then the family would come up and I handed over the eight-week-old black lab, yellow lab, golden retriever, or lab golden cross. I cannot explain how healing it is to hold an eight-week-old puppy knowing that this puppy would likely change someone's life, just as Jira had changed my life.

AT PUPPY TRUCK DAY I REMINDED THE PUPPY RAISING FAMILIES OF THE LIFE-CHANGING POWER OF GUIDE DOGS. INDEED, JIRA CHANGED MY LIFE FOR TEN YEARS. AND IN TRUTH, SHE CHANGED MY LIFE FOREVER.

At Puppy Truck Day I reminded the puppy raising families of the life-changing power of guide dogs. Indeed, Jira changed my life for ten years. And in truth, she changed my life forever. She showed me that I could navigate my surroundings safely, independently, and confidently. She empowered me with the strength to move forward even when it was hard and challenging.

During the time of intense grief after Jira died, how was I going to move forward in life? How would I yet again adjust and adapt to the new normal? I wanted nothing more than for Jira to magically come back. Unfortunately, that was not reality. Jira's life was over and her work here on earth was finished.

During those times of intense grief and adversity, we struggle to keep from sinking as the ocean waves crash over us. Reaching out to grab the anchor line takes all of our strength. We barely hang on. We need the support and courage of our family, friends, and community to hold the other end of the line and pull us to the boat. For me, during those days of overwhelming grief, the cards, emails, texts, phone calls, food, visits, prayers, counseling sessions, and sessions with Barbara, my natural health practitioner—all of these formed the anchor line that pulled me back to the boat as I grieved Jira's death.

Chapter 11

Experiencing New Life

In the two weeks that Jira was sick and in the days after she died, I did not want to entertain the thoughts I had to face. I wanted to live in denial and pretend Jira would soon come back. I was not even close to accepting life without Jira. You know those times in our lives when we experience a loss and do not want to spend a second thinking about the future and what the future might be like. The thought of adjusting to the new normal is more than we can handle. So what was the thought I had to face? Two words sum it up: new dog. The words *new dog* were extremely bad words in my vocabulary at that time. I was not ready to think about receiving a new guide dog. I just wanted Jira back, not a new dog. My friend Rebecca kept telling me, "Laura, you need to go ahead and apply for a dog because you know that it will take months before you actually receive one. Applying now does not mean you are leaving tomorrow for training." Still, the thought of applying for a new dog was overwhelming, even horrible.

Six weeks after Jira died, it was around 8 at night and I was sitting on my couch holding my laptop. With the heavy weight of grief overwhelming my body, tears flowing down my face, and anxious thoughts racing through my mind, I was filling out the online application for a new dog from The Seeing Eye. Filling out the application form was forcing me to live into my new normal. Emotionally, I was incredibly sad. Actually, it was much deeper than sadness. I also was frustrated beyond words as I was now navigating my surroundings without a guide dog. So, out of sheer frustration, I knew I had to apply. I did not want to live the rest of my life without the mobility of a guide dog. Yes, I know plenty of people who are blind, use a cane, and do very well! It is completely a choice that each person has to make. I knew for me, having a guide dog was the best choice. So, I sat there on the couch feeling such difficult emotions while also fully realizing that I had to go through the process of applying for a new dog.

Even once my application was processed, I continued to go back and forth with thoughts like, *So maybe my three references will give me horrible recommendations and they will not accept my application. Or maybe they will somehow lose my application and forget that I ever applied! Or maybe I will fail the home interview and not be accepted.* Then I would think, *But wait, I seriously need the help of a guide dog.* A few weeks after sending in my application, The Seeing Eye called to set up a home interview for January. I was relieved that the date was set and I still had about six weeks before the interview. I was glad that I was in the process of getting help. Yet I was nowhere close, emotionally, to accepting a new dog. I continued to be gripped by sadness, panic attacks, fear, and that horrible heavy feeling in my body.

As the day for the interview approached, my fear and sad-

As the day for the interview approached, my fear and sadness increased. What would the interview process be like? Yes, I had been through this interview before, but that was with a different school. Even though I knew the process would be similar, I was fearful. I was already jumping into that mind-set of, *What will the new dog be like? What if I do not like my new dog? What if the dog does not like me? What if we are not a good team?* Through the help of my family, friends, and counselor I was able to express all of these fears and then come back to being present in the moment. I was overwhelmingly sad because the reality that Jira was no longer with me was more than I could handle. She had been with me twenty-four hours a day for ten years. Of course, there were times I went places without her, but those were very few times during those ten years.

Thankfully, I made it through the interview process. It was healing for me to go through the process and know that I could in fact begin to adjust to my new normal. I was not forever going to live in this horrible place of grief that had dominated my life. But at the same time, the two-hour interview left me absolutely exhausted.

Several weeks after the interview I received a call that I had been accepted to the April 29 class at The Seeing Eye. I was instantly flooded with two opposite emotions: sadness and excitement. I was sad beyond words that I was going to have a guide dog that was not Jira. Yet I was excited that I would get my independence, freedom, and mobility back.

Remember those life jacket moments I experienced in high school? Those moments when other people were my support and strength? Those moments of support that completely held me when I was grieving while balancing the other parts of my life? Well, as we each go through horrible times of grief and loss, we need those life jacket moments. We need the actions of courage and tenacity from our family and friends so we will not sink in the waves of depression, anger, loneliness, and fear. In times of deep loss, it is not enough for others to throw us a life jacket. We need our support system to literally *be* our life jacket as we grieve while experiencing the other parts of our lives. We need the loving actions of others to support our lives as we struggle to balance working through the grief while also experiencing all the other aspects of our lives.

Just as I experienced going through the initial process of adjusting to life without sight, there is not a stop button available to us in life while we are working through the difficult emotions of grieving. We do not have the luxury of simply pressing a stop button so everything else around us halts while we experience the sadness, depression, anger, fear, and anxiety. Instead, life continues to happen all around us as we deeply grieve. In the three months after Jira died, I had several other major events occur. A few days after she passed, my papers were due for my final ordination interview. While I was already ordained as a clergy in the United Methodist Church, I had the final papers and a three-hour interview, which would mean I was ordained for life. Being the type-A personality that I am really came in handy this time! I had been working on the fifty pages of writing all summer, so everything was complete and ready to turn in. Unfortunately, I still had to prepare and go through the three-hour interview in November, just two months after Jira's passing.

Along with the ordination interview, I had several deaths in my church, other people in the church who were sick, and all the other daily responsibilities of being a pastor. On top of all that, my parents' black lab, Maggie, was diagnosed with a cancerous tumor. We got Maggie when I was in high school, so I was extremely close to her. Maggie had been such a comfort to me when Jira died. So when she was diagnosed with a cancerous tumor six weeks after Jira's passing, it was extremely difficult. Thankfully, she did live six more months. How did I survive going through that horrible time of grieving Jira while also facing all the other difficult situations? How did I not get swept away in sadness and fear? How do any of us survive those difficult times in our lives? What keeps the crashing waves of life from causing us to sink? Life jacket moments! The moments of support that others give us literally uplift our mind, body, and spirit. Just as a life jacket keeps people floating in the water, so too the support of other people keeps us floating when we would otherwise sink. For me, the support of a life jacket came through all of the cards, emails, texts, and phone calls. Receiving cards in the mail and phone calls let me know that other people were holding me in love and prayer. The food that other people brought was a life jacket. The times when people wrote or said to me, "I do not have the words, Laura. I am here for you"—these were life jacket moments. The daily text that I got from a close friend was a life jacket moment. Sarah would text me each day to let me know she was standing with me, supporting me, and holding me in prayer. She did not expect or want a text back. It was simply and powerfully her way of letting me know that even though we were hundreds of miles apart, she was there for me during this horrible time. The presence of family provided constant life jacket moments. My two-year-old niece drawing me a picture and saying, "Here, Aunt Laura, I drew a butterfly for you"—another life jacket moment. My one-year-old niece laughing that deep, pure baby laugh: a life jacket moment. Exercising and physically working out the grief was an ongoing life jacket moment! The sessions with my counselor were life jacket moments. Taking time to do mindfulness practices: life jacket moments. The appointments with Barbara, my natural health practitioner, were life jacket moments. The spiritual support from family and friends provided still more life jacket moments. Having Rebecca and other guide dog users tell me that, in fact, I was going through a normal process in grieving a first guide dog—again, life jacket moments. Needless to say, there were countless and various moments that functioned as my life jacket so that I was able to float rather than sink in these treacherous waters of life. During times of grief, loss, and adversity we need this kind of support.

With the support of our life jacket and our hands firmly grasping the anchor line, we are pulled back to the safety and security of the boat. But being pulled back and getting back into the boat does not mean life is going to be perfect, easy, and smooth. We are not exactly going to glide across a smooth surface in life. So what does being pulled back to the boat and getting back into the boat mean, we wonder? It means we are not constantly struggling to keep from being overcome by the waves of life. Rather than fighting to take each breath and struggling to stay afloat, we have the strength and courage to press on despite life's circumstances. Being in the boat means that each of the life jacket moments come together to give us the ability to move forward rather than being stuck struggling to survive in the ocean waves.

The eight months between the time Jira died and the time I went to The Seeing Eye was indeed a time when I was struggling to stay afloat. I desperately needed each life jacket moment so I could survive. But with each moment, I gained more and more strength. I gained the strength and courage to know that I could indeed adjust, yet again, to my new normal. No, life was never going to be the same, because Jira was no longer my guide dog. But yes, life could indeed move forward into the new normal.

In the weeks before I left for The Seeing Eye, I was both excited and anxious. I was excited to again receive the help I needed. Unlike the first time, when I was going to get Jira, I knew what to expect. I knew the confidence, independence, and freedom I would receive. I was ready and glad to feel like myself again. I was anxious for all the obvious reasons. I just wanted Jira back and not to have to worry about getting adjusted to another dog! I did not want to put the exhausting work into becoming another strong unit. I was anxious about trusting a new dog. Would I be able to trust this dog like I trusted Jira? Did I have the capacity to accept and love this new dog like I had Jira?

Sitting in my counselor's office working through all these deep questions and emotions, I blurted out, "I mean, what if they give me some 110-pound golden retriever that I just do not like? What would I do? I mean, that would be the end of the world!" My counselor only said one word, and it said it all. In a completely supportive but firm tone, she said, "Really?" Then she paused. I realized the ridiculousness of my question! No, actually my world would not be over if I received a 110-pound golden retriever that I did not like. With all that I had been through in my life, my world would nowhere be close to being over. With all of the trauma and difficulties in the world, I don't exactly think my world would end if I received a dog I did not like. I mean, for the first fifteen years of my life I had a huge golden retriever who I loved so much. Laughing at myself, I answered my counselor, "OK, that statement was ridiculous. I know, I know. My world would not end." But like a good counselor, she did not let me off the hook that easily! She said, "Let's work through the process of addressing the issue." So together we talked about what I would do if in fact I did receive a dog that did not work out.

As I reflect over that most difficult eight-month time of my life, I am grateful. Now you are thinking, "OK, Laura, seriously? Are you getting ready to throw out some ridiculous cliché or platitude? Are you getting ready to somehow minimize all the pain and suffering and pretend it was all good?" Of course not. So why did I say I was grateful? I am not at all grateful for the death of Jira and the sadness, fear, and anxiety that followed. What I am thankful for are the actions of love that held me when I could not hold myself. I am grateful for the actions of compassion and strength that did not allow me to sink under the rough crashing waves of loss. I am most thankful for each life jacket moment that kept me afloat. Now, was I walking around during that horrible time thinking and saying, "Oh wow, I am just so appreciative. I am thankful to each of you who are holding me in these moments." Not even close! I did not exactly feel grateful and thankful during that time. Rather, I felt sad, fearful, lonely, isolated.

During the time of intense loss and grief we are not going to be bubbling over with joy and thanksgiving. We are not going to have some amazing display of gratitude. As the life jacket moments pull us back into the boat, we can then begin to recognize our deep gratefulness. Once we are back in the boat and have the strength to live into the new normal, we can then be aware of our gratitude. Sometimes the gratefulness comes easily, naturally, and at other times it takes effort. So if gratefulness does not instantly become our dominant thought pattern, what is the purpose? What is the point of becoming aware of gratitude? Why would we go back to the moments of pain to become aware of the thankful moments?

As we think back over and continue through the grieving process, being aware of our gratitude provides deep healing to our mind and spirit. Recognizing those moments and actions of courage and love from friends and family shows us that, indeed, we were not grieving and going through that horrible process alone. What healing comes when we can know that we were, and will, continue to be supported! Becoming grateful for the moments of support does not begin to minimize or take away from the pain of the situation. Being grateful for the support shows us that the horrible situation does not permanently crush and destroy our spirits. We made it through the difficult time of loss and will have the strength to adjust to the new normal.

> AS WE THINK BACK OVER AND CONTINUE THROUGH THE GRIEVING PROCESS, BEING AWARE OF OUR GRATITUDE PROVIDES DEEP HEALING TO OUR MIND AND SPIRIT.

An example of being aware of gratitude took place while I was presenting at a class retreat. Before Jira died, I was asked to be one of the presenters and facilitators for a class retreat at Princeton Theological Seminary. I was honored to be asked, so, of course, I agreed. Once Jira died and I experienced the months that followed, I seriously considered telling the school that I could not attend. However, I did not cancel. March rolled around and it was time for me to leave for the event. But wait—there was one major difference. Jira was not with me. The one who had guided me for so many years was not there. Jira and I knew the campus so well after being there for three years, and now I was not going to have her help. I knew that I would have so much support and be surrounded by friends while at Princeton, so I did not cancel. I did have more than the support I needed. How healing it was to be around friends who knew Jira so well and were sad she had died. After all, Jira had received her masters in dogmatics! While it was healing and wonderful to be with friends, it was also sad and unbelievably difficult. Being in a place I knew so well and yet not being able to navigate like normal was incredibly frustrating. I realized even more what Jira did for me and how she empowered me to navigate with confidence.

One of my close friends from school was part of the class. The first night several of us were sitting at a table in the dining area. Everyone got up to leave except Allison and me. She turned to me and asked, "How are you doing?" It was one of those moments that said, "We are close friends. So I *really mean*: how are you doing?" Without thinking about it, knowing that I could be totally honest, I stopped eating, turned toward Allison, and said,

"It is like I am sitting at the bottom of the Grand Canyon and somehow have to climb my way out." Without hesitating, Allison said, "I cannot begin to know what you are going through. I just want you to know that I am sitting down there at the bottom with you." Before I had a chance to respond, several people walked up to the table, so our conversation was over. But there was no more that needed to be said anyway. In one sentence I shared how I was doing, and in one sentence Allison said that she was right there with me in the pain. And that was enough.

IN ONE SENTENCE I SHARED HOW I WAS DOING, AND IN ONE SENTENCE ALLISON SAID THAT SHE WAS RIGHT THERE WITH ME IN THE PAIN. AND THAT WAS ENOUGH.

During the trip and afterward, I was not exactly filled with appreciation for the experience, or for Allison's words. As I worked to be aware of those grateful moments, I grew to a place of becoming overwhelmingly thankful for that Princeton trip. I am grateful for all the actions of love and compassion. I am most thankful for the friends who supported me with hospitality that was healing to my spirit. I am thankful for the friends who laughed and cried with me. I am grateful for the opportunity to realize just how much my life is strengthened and empowered through the work of a guide dog. I am grateful for the gift of being honest with a friend and her being willing to sit in the struggle with me. Did I feel grateful in that moment? In truth, no. But has that experience brought healing to my mind and spirit as I adjust to the new normal? Absolutely!

* * * * * * *

The eight months between Jira dying and going to The Seeing Eye had come and gone. April 29 arrived and I found myself unpacking my suitcase. Just like at Guide Dogs for the Blind, one of the trainers was orienting me to my room, and I could not focus on a word she was saying. The strong emotion of sadness flowed through my mind, body, and spirit. There was no turning back now. I was at The Seeing Eye to receive a new dog. From the moment of arriving through the next few days, I was overwhelmed with sadness and tears. I tried hard to remember the words of my counselor, who told me to turn toward my emotions and acknowledge what I was feeling. Well, rest assured, I totally mastered that skill! I seemed to be nothing but a ball of tears. For example, we were all sitting in the conference room on the first full day when one of the trainers said, "Now you are going to get your new leashes." Then a few minutes later a trainer handed me a brand new leash and said, "Here is the leash for the dog that you will receive tomorrow." Without responding, I sank down in my chair, holding the new leash awkwardly while the tears started flowing. I could not stop them even if I tried. Thankfully, the school is well prepared for people receiving their second dog. There is actually a name for the difficult process of losing your first guide dog and receiving your second! It is called second dog syndrome. It is a well-known process for all guide dog users. So the trainers were incredibly supportive and gave me the space to experience sadness and tears.

Wednesday morning arrived, and that meant dog day—the day I would be receiving my new dog. After breakfast and a short lecture, each person in the class went back to their rooms to wait. Each of our trainers would come to our room with the new dog. I was pacing in my room, feeling numb. I could hear the dogs barking. Just like when I was at Guide Dogs for the Blind, I thought to myself, *One of those barking dogs is going to be my new eyes.* As I was pacing back and forth, about 9 a.m., there was a knock on my door. Shaking so hard that I could barely open the door, I opened it and my trainer said, "I have your new dog, Laura." I started shaking even harder. I walked about ten steps to the chair and sat down. The trainer then said, "Laura, meet your new dog, Betty. She is a black lab." Shaking, sitting there in the chair, my first thought was, *What? A female black lab?* OK, so maybe the word running through my head was not "what"! Rather, there were a number of other four-letter words! You get the point! I thought, *Oh no, this is going to be even more difficult since she is also a black lab.* Shaking and with tears running down my face, I said, "Hey, Betty." The tears continued to flow as I petted her head and ears. The trainer took her leash off Betty, put my new leash on her, and handed me the leash. She said, "Spend time playing with Betty, and I will be back to get you for your first walk."

Before she left my room, the trainer turned and said, "Oh, I just want you to know that her name is Betty because she is named after the famous actress Betty White. Betty generously supports The Seeing Eye. So in honor of her 90th birthday, the school decided to name a dog in her honor, and this is the dog."

After my trainer left I sat down on the floor to play with Betty. I am sure she thought I had never been around a dog before. I was still shaking, crying, and trying to pretend I wanted to be around this dog. Thankfully, she was completely different than Jira. She was taller, longer, and had a more narrow face. While I played with her I called my parents, brother, and a few friends to let them know I had received my new dog. You would have thought I was calling to deliver some horrible, sad news. I mean, there was just no excitement or joy in my voice. I still just wanted Jira back.

I STILL JUST WANTED JIRA BACK.

After what seemed like forever, the trainer came to get me for my first walk. Once we were outside, I put the harness on Betty. I then picked up the harness handle, put the leash around my left hand, and gave Betty the command to walk forward. For the first time, I was walking with this new dog as my guide. With the trainer beside me, I walked for a few minutes around the obstacle course that was set up for each person to walk with their dog. As we walked the trainer asked how it felt. With tears of joy and thanksgiving I said, "I feel human again!" In no way was I through with the difficult transition of adjusting from Jira to Betty. However, I was excited to again walk with confidence and ease.

Over the next three weeks I went through the difficult and yet exciting process of learning Betty's personality and the two of us learning how to be a strong unit together. There were still moments of tears and sadness when I just wanted Jira back. Thankfully, the school provided a counselor to work with each of us who were going through second dog syndrome. We had group sessions as well as individual sessions to support us as we transitioned. As I worked through the difficult emotions, I also experienced healing emotions. Remember how my first full walk with Jira was in the rain? Well, I am not kidding when I say that my first walk with Betty was in the rain! For the first few walks with our new dogs the trainer also was holding a leash. Then after a few walks we were completely on our own. The morning I was set for my first walk with Betty, it was pouring rain. I do not mean just a few drizzles; it was a soaking, hard rain! I stood in this downpour and gave Betty the command to go forward. Even though we were both soaking wet after 30 seconds, I did not mind! I could have walked for hours and hours in that driving rain. Why? Because I felt like myself again. I was walking with complete confidence and independence. After a few blocks of walking in the rain, large puddles splashing over me, and feeling Betty's strong pull, I knew I was going to be just fine. Yes, adjusting to the new normal was difficult, even miserable. But yes, I could indeed adjust to the new normal that was my seeing eye dog, Betty.

> I COULD HAVE WALKED FOR HOURS AND HOURS IN THAT DRIVING RAIN. WHY? BECAUSE I FELT LIKE MYSELF AGAIN. I WAS WALKING WITH COMPLETE CONFIDENCE AND INDEPENDENCE.

The first walk with Betty in that rain showed me I was able to display the courage and strength needed to adjust and live into the new normal. There was also another walk with Betty that showed me I could work with another dog. During the last week of school I went to New York City with my trainer. Since it was my second time going to the city with Betty, I felt like a pro. You know those times when you think, and even say, "Oh, I have totally got this!" Those times when we are way too confident and think we cannot learn anything? Well, this was one of those moments. Thinking I did not need to know anything new, I was walking confidently and smoothly through America's busiest city. I loved the wall-to-wall people, loud sounds, and taxi drivers. Well, maybe not all of the taxi drivers! I came to a street corner and waited for my trainer and another student in the class. Once they were with me, I listened for the flow of traffic. Once I thought it was safe, I started across the street. About halfway across, Betty completely stopped. A few seconds later a car went flying by in front of us. I froze. Well, let me tell you that freezing in the middle of a New York City street is not a good idea! My trainer ran up to me and said, "Keep walking!" As we finished walking across the street, she said, "Betty did great in that situation. She saw the car coming and stopped you from danger." Again, just like that moment on a busy street corner with Jira in San Francisco, I knew I could trust Betty. As I walked another block, I knew I could deeply trust Betty. Just like with Jira, I knew that Betty now could indeed be my eyes.

* * * * * * *

In times of grieving and loss, we go through the most difficult periods, including feeling like we are just barely surviving. We depend on those life jacket moments of courage and support to be our strength. As each life jacket moment gives us endurance, we are then able to survive—and more than just survive. We are able to live as people with value and purpose. We are able to yet again adjust and move forward. The adjustment is hard, uncomfortable. We resist the new normal because we want life just as it was before the loss. Unfortunately, going back to the previous way of life is not possible. Our choices are to live into the new normal or remain in a constant place of depression and anxiety. Often it seems easier, maybe even better, to remain in a place of sadness and fear. Yet acknowledging our difficult emotions, feeling those emotions, and choosing to continue living is a much more healthy and fulfilling place to live. What courage and strength it requires to choose to move forward. Adjusting to the new normal is just like the old saying, "One step forward and two steps back." Adapting to our new reality often seems as if we are not making any progress. But after countless times of choosing strength and tenacity, we develop the ability to accept our new normal and embrace our current lives.

> UNFORTUNATELY, GOING BACK TO THE PREVIOUS WAY OF LIFE IS NOT POSSIBLE. OUR CHOICES ARE TO LIVE INTO THE NEW NORMAL OR REMAIN IN A CONSTANT PLACE OF DEPRESSION AND ANXIETY.

On both my first walk with Jira and my first walk with Betty, it was raining and anything but a nice, beautiful day. As I walked with each of them, I was wet, muddy, and cold. I was also uncertain and unsure about the new normal. Jira and Betty gave me a life of confidence and freedom. For each of our lives, adjusting to the new normal is like that first walk in the rain. With the loving actions of others, we can continue walking through the wet, muddy, and cold experiences—and these ultimately lead to empowerment and gratefulness.

Chapter 12

Different, Yet Empowered

The empowerment and freedom I experienced through Betty was healing and brought life to my spirit. Adapting yet again to a new normal was not quick, easy, or smooth. There were moments of complete joy, such as being able to navigate independently at a conference just a few weeks after being home from The Seeing Eye. Then there were moments of incredible frustration as Betty and I learned to be a strong unit. Through the moments of joy as well as the frustrating moments, Betty showed me that indeed life can continue forward.

Two weeks after I was home from The Seeing Eye, a woman in our church died. A few days later I was conducting the funeral and graveside services. After the funeral home service, we were all gathered at the graveside. It was a very hot June day. About halfway through the service I was praying, and Betty started chewing a magnolia leaf that was on the ground. Now, Jira and I were so connected that I could just barely tug on her leash. This tug said to her, "You better stop right now, young lady!" And Jira knew, just through my energy, what I was saying. I did not have to say a word or even look in her direction. However, with Betty it was a completely different story! I had only known her for six weeks at that point. So what was I going to do? I could not exactly stop to correct my dog in the middle of my prayer for this ninety-three-year-old woman. I had to keep going with the prayer. But each chew brought a louder and louder crunching sound. Even though I was mortified, I had to continue forward with the rest of the service as though nothing was happening. Once the service was over I was speaking to each of the family members. No one said a word about Betty crunching down on that leaf. So I thought maybe, somehow, they were so focused on the prayer that they just did not notice!

A few days later I called the children of this woman. As I was talking to the daughter, she said to me, "Pastor, I have to tell you about your dog eating the magnolia leaf." I immediately thought, *Oh no! This is going to be bad. She is going to say that my dog totally ruined her mother's graveside service. . . . Well, I better say something before she says anything.* So I began with, "Oh, I am sorry that my dog was chewing on that leaf. I know that was horribly distracting for you and your family at such a difficult time." Much to my surprise, she started laughing and said, "No! Actually it was a gift." I thought, *A gift? Seriously?* That is not even close to anything I was thinking in the moment. But she went on to say, "You know, when your dog started chewing on the leaf, I looked up at her and she was calmly eating away at that big, thick green leaf. Pastor, in that moment my mother was telling me through your dog that life can continue on. There was just something about the way your dog was chewing on the leaf that said to me: life can continue going." Sitting in my office on the phone talking to

LIFE DID INDEED CONTINUE FOR ME AS I MADE THE TRANSITION FROM JIRA TO BETTY. LIFE CAN, IN FACT, CONTINUE FOR EACH OF OUR LIVES REGARDLESS OF THE SITUATION.

the daughter of the woman who just died, I knew she was right. Life could continue for the family even as they grieved their ninety-three-year-old mother and grandmother. Life did indeed continue for me as I made the transition from Jira to Betty. Life can, in fact, continue for each of our lives regardless of the situation.

On that hot June day standing at the graveside, the grieving family learned a powerful lesson. As the pastor conducting the service, I learned a powerful lesson. For each of us, we can all learn these powerful lessons. Throughout each of our lives we will experience times of adversity, challenges, and obstacles, both personally and professionally. Some of the challenges will be no more than minor annoyances and inconveniences. Other adversities will greatly impact our lives. Then there will be those moments of deep trauma that absolutely rock us to the core of our being. The situation is so great that every part of our life is directly affected. We wonder if we can survive. We ask ourselves questions such as: Is life worth living? What am I doing here? Is the effort worth it? Will life ever be better? Our day-to-day lives can be such a struggle that we question our existence.

Being born with complete sight and then experiencing the trauma of adjusting to life without sight has been incredibly difficult. Constantly adapting to each new stage has been overwhelming to say the least. Living into each new normal is exhausting. Being a person who is labeled different is exhausting. The comments I receive from other people are often degrading, belittling, and just downright strange! I could write an entire book on the unbelievable comments that I receive from people! For example, I was eating dinner one night with my family at a restaurant as we celebrated my cousin's birthday. There were about ten of us gathered at a long table eating and talking. Once we were finished, a woman came up to me, put her hand on my shoulder, and said, "Honey, I want you to know that I think you are just amazing." I looked up at the lady as if to say, "Wait? Who in the world are you?" She then went on to say, "I have been watching you and your dog. I have watched you eat your whole meal and you are just amazing. I am just shocked that you were able to leave the house and come out to dinner with these other people and eat. You are just amazing." Then she turned and walked away. Now, let me make it clear about the tone this woman displayed. She had a deep, southern voice and each word took about four times the number of syllables that word needed! So to say that each word was drawn out was an understatement! But the deep, southern drawl was not the problem. The problem was the pity in her voice as she spoke each word. Though I am sure she did not mean to offend me, I was so shocked by her words that I didn't have a response. I mean, how do you respond to that type of comment? In the moments that followed I experienced a range of emotions, from anger to sadness to just laughing at the poor woman's ridiculous comments. I said to my family, "Well, what do you think she would have said if I told her I was a pastor?"

I cannot begin to count the times that people walk up to me and, with all pity, say, "You are just amazing." Now, they are not saying that because they know me. They are not saying that because of some quality I have or some goal I have reached. They are telling me I am amazing because I have a disability and I am out in the world living and breathing. Then, there is one comment that will stay with me for a long time. I was at a conference and a man walked up to me and said, "Do you know what color your dog is?" Now, this man knew that I was a clergy. He knew that I had a masters level education. He himself was a highly educated person and had an extremely important position within an international organization. No, he was not joking or trying to be funny. He seriously asked me if I knew the color of my dog! Again, I was shocked. All I could get out was, "Yes." Then just like the time at the restaurant, I became angry, sad, and frustrated. The entire range of comments I receive as a person with a disability can be discouraging and emotionally exhausting.

Between the effort of living life as a person with a disability and receiving all of the difficult comments, life can seem overwhelming. I can wonder, *Just what is the point of the effort? Why do I keep going?* Some days I just want to pull the covers up over my head and not even attempt to get up. I want to go far away and forget this thing called life. Believing the mantra that I repeated over and over to myself during middle school—"I cannot. I cannot"—this seems correct. So why continue the effort? Why do I throw off the covers and yet again tackle another day? Just as life has been difficult, overwhelming, and exhausting, life also has been empowering.

JUST AS LIFE HAS BEEN DIFFICULT, OVERWHELMING, AND EXHAUSTING, LIFE ALSO HAS BEEN EMPOWERING.

As I could write a book on the hurtful comments I have received, I could also write an entire book on the encouraging comments and actions. For example, I was at a rehearsal dinner for a friend whose wedding I was officiating. At the dinner, I was sitting next to Rachel and across from her three-year-old-daughter, Meredith. "So, Meredith, are you excited about being in the wedding tomorrow?" I asked her. As most three-year-olds would, she shook her head as if to say yes. Well, obviously, that did not do me much good! Without hesitating, and in a completely normal tone of voice, Rachel said to her daughter, "Remember that Laura sees through words." Then Meredith said to me, "Yes, ma'am." Then we continued with our conversation. I cannot fully explain how empowered I felt in that moment. Without making a scene or even changing the tone of her voice, Rachel reminded her daughter that I could not see her shaking her head. I felt fully human because Rachel and Meredith were relating to me as a complete human being. They were fully acknowledging my disability while also fully acknowledging my humanity.

> I FELT FULLY HUMAN BECAUSE RACHEL AND MEREDITH WERE RELATING TO ME AS A COMPLETE HUMAN BEING.

Then there was the trip to visit my cousins. My cousin, his wife, and two daughters lived twelve hundred miles away. I flew out to spend a long weekend at their house. Once they picked me up at the airport, we went to their house before going out to a late lunch. After walking in the door, my cousin Elizabeth said, "Laura, I want to show you around the house since this is the first time you have been here." So I am thinking, *Oh, she is going to show me and tell me about all of the pretty decorations in her house.* Elizabeth then began at the front door and described the layout of her house. We walked room by room while she perfectly described each living space. Once we walked through the house, we went into the backyard and she showed me the pool and furniture. Then we walked back through the house and she showed me the front yard, where I could take Betty to the bathroom. After a complete tour of the house, Elizabeth said, "Now you can make yourself at home since you know the layout." I thought to myself, *Whoa, girl! You are good! I mean, you have known me only a few years since you married my cousin.* Only one word is needed to describe that experience: empowerment! I felt totally empowered because I could navigate their house independently. For the next few days, I did not have to depend on them to help me get around the house. I have had similar experiences at close friends' houses when they also showed me around their house so I would be comfortable walking around safely. Elizabeth and other friends orienting me to their houses showed me that they are relating to me as a full person. Just like Rachel, they were fully acknowledging my disability while also fully acknowledging my humanity.

Then there were moments of empowerment through another cousin's communications with me. Shannon and her husband have two young sons. When she sends pictures of their children to family, obviously, I cannot view those pictures. So what does she do? She sends me a video describing the pictures. When her oldest son was too small to talk, she would describe what he was doing. Then once he could talk, she would have her son describe to me, from the video, what he was doing. Even as I was writing this, I got a new text message. I reached over, grabbed my phone, and realized it was a text from Shannon. She had sent me a video of her boys laughing as they were playing together. Literally, as I was writing about the empowerment that I received from Shannon and her text messages, I received another text from her! Just another one of those moments you cannot plan. You can only smile and say, "Thank you." Shannon realized I could not benefit from the pictures she sent. So rather than feeling sorry for me or just saying, "Oh well," she found a way to meet me where I am.

There is one question I receive both from people I know

and complete strangers, and it is most helpful. The question is: "How can I best help you?" Why do I love this question? Why does this question give life to my spirit? Through the question each person is acknowledging that he or she does not know the best way to help me in a particular situation. The person is also acknowledging that he or she is willing to help me in the best way possible. Finally, the person is acknowledging that I am a human being who knows my limits as well as knows my needs. There is absolutely no way every person can know when I need help and when I do not need help. I do not even pretend to expect others to know how and when I need help. What I do expect is for people to have the courage to treat me as a full human and be willing to ask how best they can help.

As I receive comments and actions that are degrading and belittling, as well as comments and actions that are empowering and encouraging, I face a choice. I have a choice each day. Am I going to allow the negative, hurtful comments to control my life? Or am I going to allow the positive comments to propel me to continue on with life? Actually, the answer is not as simple as making one choice over the other. The decision is not as easy as saying to myself, *Oh, I am just going to live believing those horrible, negative comments.* Nor is it a matter of: *Oh, I am just going to completely ignore those degrading comments and only listen to the good comments.* What is the answer? Rather than my decision being one extreme or the other, the answer to the two questions lies in the tension of living into both choices.

What does living into the tension of both choices mean? Dwelling on the hurtful comments is not a healthy place to live. Allowing belittling comments to dominate my life will not exactly help me live to my full potential. At the same time, choosing to only listen to the empowering comments is not healthy either. Allowing myself to only focus on the good comments also prevents me from living into my full potential. For example, when I was eating dinner with my family at the restaurant and received such hurtful comments, I had a choice. I could choose to agree with the lady and be absolutely shocked that I was able to leave the house and eat dinner like anyone else! I could choose to allow the lady's comments to speak truth in my life. I could go home and decide to stay home and not be an active part of the world. Second, I could choose to hear the lady's comments and completely ignore everything she said. I could have just kept talking to my family like the lady never existed. Or, I had a third choice. I could choose to hear the lady's comments and feel the deep hurt, frustration, and anger. I could express to my family how incredibly frustrating it is to receive those types of comments. Then I could choose to let those feelings go and listen to my own empowering words and those of my family. Indeed, I know I am more than capable of being out of the house and interacting in the world. My family constantly tells me through their words and actions that they also believe I have the ability to be out of the house interacting with the world. Acknowledging the difficult comments, feeling my emotions, and choosing to receive the comments of empowerment is the choice that is healthy and healing.

> OR, I HAD A THIRD CHOICE. I COULD CHOOSE TO HEAR THE LADY'S COMMENTS AND FEEL THE DEEP HURT, FRUSTRATION, AND ANGER. I COULD EXPRESS TO MY FAMILY HOW INCREDIBLY FRUSTRATING IT IS TO RECEIVE THOSE TYPES OF COMMENTS.

Deciding to live into the tension of both choices is life-giving for me as well as all of our lives. What life is given to our spirits when we choose to acknowledge the difficult situations, feel the emotions, and choose to receive empowering comments. We all know that life is hard. Life is difficult. Life is confusing. Life is messy. Life can be downright strange! As we each receive comments and actions that are hurtful, harmful, healing, and encouraging, we can swing from having zero self-confidence to thinking we are the greatest thing ever created. How do we stay balanced? We do so by choosing to live into the tension of acknowledging the difficulties as well as acknowledging and living into the encouragement.

But there is one problem! Choosing to live into the tension of receiving the positive and negative comments is hard work! It does *not* come naturally. At least not for me! Some days I just want to say to the lady at the restaurant, "OK, so you are right. I should not be out contributing to the world." Other days I want to say, "OK, lady, I will show you! Watch me be the most productive person in the world just to prove you wrong." Living into the tension of both choices takes vulnerability, courage, and strength. Vulnerability is required so we can be in the uncomfortable place of acknowledging the difficult comments! How vulnerable it feels to receive those hurtful and harmful comments and actions! What courage is needed to feel the range of emotions! While it is easy to react in one extreme or the other, it takes courage to allow ourselves the space to feel the emotions and not react. Then incredible strength is required to choose to believe the positive statements about our lives. And this process must repeat itself again and again. We will not one time make

CHOOSING TO LIVE INTO THE TENSION OF RECEIVING THE POSITIVE AND NEGATIVE COMMENTS IS HARD WORK! IT DOES *NOT* COME NATURALLY.

the decision to live in the healthy tension and then for the rest of our lives automatically default to that decision. Rather, we daily face the choice to live into the vulnerability, courage, and strength that leads to empowerment.

Living a life that embraces vulnerability, courage, and strength takes a combination of grit and gratitude. Living into daily grit gives us the ability to remain grounded as we experience those times of adversity and trauma as well as moments of joy and laughter. Having the grit of determination and perseverance gives us the strength to live into the tension of those moments that are discouraging as well as the moments that are encouraging. The good news is that we are not struggling to display daily grit on our own. Rather, having daily grit means we are able to access the tenacity of others. We are able to draw strength from the grit that surrounds our lives.

In the first days when I was diagnosed with a retinal disease, grit came through the perseverance displayed by my parents. They showed incredible grit as they researched and did all they could to learn about resources that would help me continue living a full life. Grit also came through my brother; Rob was determined to treat me as a normal sister and tell me that giving up was just not a choice. Grit came through my extended family as they surrounded me with strength through their love and prayers. Grit came through my community as they also surrounded me with love and support. Grit literally and figuratively came through the process of having a guide dog, which enabled me to move forward. Grit came through complete strangers who offered words of strength and hope. Grit came through my friends who acknowledged me as fully human. There have absolutely been times when I felt like I was thrown into the deep ocean water while huge waves crashed over my head. Life seemed like I was all alone, fighting for my very survival. Even though I felt all alone and isolated, I was surrounded by the grit of others. The determination, courage, and perseverance of family, friends, and community supported me with actions of grit.

I experienced those words and actions of grit in the first months and years after I was diagnosed. Thankfully, the supportive words and actions did not stop. Instead, the determination and perseverance of others continues each day. I have the daily choice of accessing the courageous actions that surround my life. I also have the choice of allowing the grit of others to provide me the courage and tenacity I need for myself. So I am not depending solely on other people to display grit for me; rather, I am choosing strength and courage. What a strong force is created when we can each depend on the determination and perseverance of other people as well as our own courageous actions. No, we will not be immune to the difficulties and messiness of life. But yes, we will in fact have what we need to work through and overcome those moments of adversity.

GRATEFULNESS GIVES US THE OPPORTUNITY TO BE AWARE OF THE SUPPORTIVE ACTIONS THAT HOLD US IN DIFFICULT MOMENTS.

Along with grit, the gift of gratitude gives us strength. Through gratitude we are able to live a life centered on the loving actions that surround our lives. Gratitude also allows us to focus on what we have rather than what we do not have. Gratefulness gives us the opportunity to be aware of the supportive actions that hold us in difficult moments. Now, all that sounds well and good. But how do we live this life of gratitude? Does it just happen? Is there one big moment where we say, "OK world, I am going to live a life of gratitude!"—and it just happens? Absolutely not! Cultivating a life of gratitude starts with choosing to become aware of those people and moments that cause us to say thank you. We recognize that the people and events in our lives give us the ability to live into our full potential. Gratitude also means that we are thankful for the people and situations that allow us to overcome struggles.

Living a life of gratitude can be expressed in many different ways. Through our words we can say "thank you" to those around us, as well as to complete strangers. We can write down the people, events, and situations we are grateful for each day. We can live a life of gratitude by showing kind actions. The ways to express our gratitude are endless. Just like a seed that is planted, living a life of gratefulness starts by that one small action of gratitude. Then, just as a seed grows into a large plant, so too will our actions of gratefulness grow into a life of gratitude.

Sometimes gratitude is easy and doesn't take much effort. For example, it was easy to be most grateful for the time my close friend Lindsey spent with me on my birthday. At the time we were living two hours away. The timing was not exactly optimal for Lindsey. She was at the end of packing up her house to move. Just two days after my birthday she and her husband were moving seven hundred miles for a new job. Driving two hours to spend the day with me before moving was not exactly the best for her! So, I was incredibly grateful that Lindsey took the time and made the effort to come for my birthday. Being grateful for her gift of presence did not take much effort.

Then there are those times when being grateful is anything but easy. In the midst of adversity and difficulties I am not exactly feeling thankful. Being diagnosed with an eye disease and living through the extremely difficult years of middle school and high school, I was not exactly bubbling over with thanksgiving and joy. I could not find anything to be thankful for in my life. In those moments I was too overwhelmed with my circumstances to be thankful. Once I was past those harsh years, however, I became deeply grateful for the love and support that I had received physically, emotionally, and spiritually. And becoming aware of that gratitude was incredibly healing.

Similarly, going through the intense grieving process after Jira died, I was not anywhere close to living in gratitude. Thinking back over that horrible time, however, I recognize the endless actions that now make me grateful. For example, my close friend, Molly, sent me a card each week reminding me that she was thinking of me and supporting me. It might not seem a big deal to put a card in the mail. But her cards were just not any cards. Molly figured out how to braille out the words she wanted to write. Was it perfect? No; in fact, we would both get a huge laugh when I would call her to say, "OK, now what was that word? I tried and tried, but I still could not figure it out!" Molly spent numerous hours researching and making each card that she sent. The braille cards I received each week gave me strength beyond strength. Was it easy to be grateful as I grieved Jira? Of course not. Am I overwhelmed with gratitude for the loving actions that supported me during a horrible time? Absolutely!

Cultivating a life of gratitude is a daily process. Expressing our gratefulness both when life is easy and when life is difficult brings healing and strength. Choosing to plant that first seed of thankfulness will grow into a large, strong plant as, day by day, we each choose to live a life of gratitude.

* * * * * * *

As a three-year-old, I stood on stage dressed in my pink leotard, pink tutu, and ballet shoes ready for the dance recital to begin. When I realized that the other children were frozen in place and not dancing, I decided to lead them! My outgoing and fearless self did what I needed to do so the dance could continue. I think it's safe to say my three-year-old self, my parents, brother, grandmothers, and everyone else sitting in the audience never entertained the thought that I would one day desperately need that same spirit so the dance of life could continue for me.

I THINK IT'S SAFE TO SAY MY THREE-YEAR-OLD SELF, MY PARENTS, BROTHER, GRANDMOTHERS, AND EVERYONE ELSE SITTING IN THE AUDIENCE NEVER ENTERTAINED THE THOUGHT THAT I WOULD ONE DAY DESPERATELY NEED THAT SAME SPIRIT SO THE DANCE OF LIFE COULD CONTINUE FOR ME.

Just as those other children were frozen in place at the thought of performing their dance in front of a crowd, so too I was frozen in place when I was faced with the reality that I would become blind. Just like those children, I was stopped dead in my tracks. How could the show of life continue? The lights were on, the music had started, and it was show time. Yet I was not ready for the show of my life to continue.

I had to face, head on, the reality of adapting to life without sight. I had to resist the temptation to tell myself, over and over, "I cannot. I cannot." Just as I fearlessly led the three-year-old dance recital, I needed other people to fearlessly lead me as I went through the trauma of adjusting to life without sight. I needed the grit of strength, determination, and tenacity to lead me, hold me, and support me as I faced the days ahead. The other three-year-old children were able to start the dance they knew so well once they had a leader reminding them of each step. So, too, I was able to again start the dance of life once I had the strong example of courage and perseverance. Then things reached the point in the three-year-old dance recital when there *was no* leader and follower. All of us were once again dancing together in the dance we knew so well. It's this way in life: there comes a point when the actions of the grit displayed by others and the actions of grit shown by myself blend together so the full dance of life can be lived out.

The dance of my life is not complete. The lights are still on, the music is still playing, and it continues to be show time. I know there will yet be moments when I will be like that three-year-old child, fearlessly leading while others are frozen in place. There will also be those moments when I will be frozen in place and desperately needing fearless leadership from others. There will be times when I love life and am filled with joy. Then there will be times when I am so overwhelmed by the difficulties of life that I do not want to face another day. While I do not even pretend to have this thing called life figured out, I do know the tools I need to live through the ups and downs of life. Physically, emotionally, and spiritually, I need the balance of grit and gratitude.

> THE DANCE OF MY LIFE IS NOT COMPLETE. THE LIGHTS ARE STILL ON, THE MUSIC IS STILL PLAYING, AND IT CONTINUES TO BE SHOW TIME.

Actually, the tools I need to survive and thrive in life are not unique to me. We all need the resources of grit and gratitude in our mind, body, and spirit. We will all face unbelievable challenges and obstacles as well as times of happiness and joy. As we experience our lives and face our future, our lives just might look like that three-year-old dance recital. At times we will be the strong, courageous person who is able to move forward while also helping others to show the same strength and courage. Then there will be those times when we are frozen by difficult circumstances. We are completely dependent on others to show us determination and perseverance. There will be those times where we are living in the balance of receiving and showing others how to live the dance of courage and strength. Just as we each live the dance of courage and strength, we can also live the dance of gratitude. Sometimes we will be the one expressing our deep gratefulness. Other times, we will need

> JUST AS WE EACH LIVE THE DANCE OF COURAGE AND STRENGTH, WE CAN ALSO LIVE THE DANCE OF GRATITUDE.

people to demonstrate what it means to live a life of gratitude.

So we each have a choice. We cannot choose many of the circumstances that occur in our life. However, we can choose how we respond. We can choose to allow the struggles and difficulties of life to define us. Or we can choose to respond to our life circumstances in a way that allows us to live into our full potential. We can choose to respond in a way that blocks the gifts we are able to give to the world. Or we can choose to respond in a way that allows our gifts to be fully received by the world.

The choice is ours. Which will we choose? Together, let us choose to be like that three-year-old dance class. The lights are on, the music is playing, and it is show time. Even though the dance may not come naturally or smoothly, together we can figure out how to complete the steps. Now is our show time. Together, let's live life as we apply grit and experience gratitude!

Connect with the Author

Laura Bratton is the founder of Ubi Global, LLC. The mission of Ubi Global is to provide inspirational speaking and coaching sessions that empower all people to overcome challenges and obstacles with grit and gratitude.

You can connect with Laura at:

Website: www.ubiglobal.org

Facebook: www.facebook.com/UBI-Global

Twitter: www.twitter.com/LauraRBratton

LinkedIn: find Laura at www.linkedin.com: Laura Bratton, inspirational speaker and coach at UBI Global.

Endnotes

1. http://www.merriam-webster.com/dictionary/grit

2. Angela Lee Duckworth, TED Talk: "The Key to Success? Grit." April 2013. Copyright TED Conferences LLC. https://www.ted.com/talks/angela_lee_duckworth_the_key_to_success_grit?language=en (accessed May 6, 2016).

3. David Steindl-Rast, TED Talk: "Want to Be Happy? Be Grateful." June 2013. Copyright TED Conferences LLC. https://www.ted.com/talks/david_steindl_rast_want_to_be_happy_be_grateful?language=en (accessed May 6, 2016).

4. Brene Brown, *Daring Greatly: How the Courage to Be Vulnerable Transforms the Way We Live, Love, Parent, and Lead* (New York: Avery, 2012, 2015).

5. Quotations from Terri, disability coordinator, used by permission. Email sent to author, May 25, 2016.

6. Brene Brown, *Rising Strong: The Reckoning, The Rumble, The Revolution* (New York: Spiegel & Grau, 2015).

7. Quotations from Dr. Brown used by permission. Email sent to author, May 26, 2016.

8. Quotations from Jana used by permission. Email sent to author, May 25, 2016.

9. Quotations from Dr. Griesel used by permission. Email sent to author, May 26, 2016.

10. Quotations from Tammy used by permission. Email sent to author, May 25, 2016.